Foundations of Intellectual Freedom

ALA Neal-Schuman purchases fund advocacy, awareness,
and accreditation programs for library professionals worldwide.

Foundations of Intellectual Freedom

Emily J. M. Knox

CHICAGO :: 2023

EMILY J. M. KNOX is an associate professor in the School of Information Sciences at the University of Illinois at Urbana-Champaign. Her book *Book Banning in 21st-Century America* was published by Rowman and Littlefield and is the first monograph in the Beta Phi Mu Scholars Series. She is also the editor of *Trigger Warnings: History, Theory Context* (Rowman and Littlefield) and is coeditor of *Foundations of Information Ethics* (ALA Neal-Schuman). Her articles have been published in *Library Quarterly*, *Library and Information Science Research*, and the *Journal of Intellectual Freedom and Privacy*. Dr. Knox has served on the boards of the Association for Information Science and Technology, the Freedom to Read Foundation, and the National Coalition Against Censorship. Her research interests include information access, intellectual freedom and censorship, information ethics, information policy, and the intersection of print culture and reading practices. She is also a member of the Mapping Information Access research team. She received her PhD from the Rutgers University School of Communication and Information. Her master's degree in library and information science is from the iSchool at Illinois. She also holds a BA in religious studies from Smith College and an AM in the same field from the University of Chicago Divinity School.

© 2023 by Emily J. M. Knox

Extensive effort has gone into ensuring the reliability of the information in this book; however, the publisher makes no warranty, express or implied, with respect to the material contained herein.

ISBNs
978-0-8389-3783-9 (paper)
978-0-8389-3745-7 (PDF)
978-0-8389-3825-6 (ePub)

Library of Congress Cataloging-in-Publication Data
Names: Knox, Emily, 1976- author.
Title: Foundations of intellectual freedom / Emily J. M. Knox.
Description: Chicago : ALA Neal-Schuman, 2023. | Includes bibliographical references and
   index. | Summary: "Designed to function as both an introductory text for LIS students as well as a complementary resource for current professionals, this book provides a cohesive, holistic perspective on intellectual freedom"—Provided by publisher.
Identifiers: LCCN 2022028169 (print) | LCCN 2022028170 (ebook) | ISBN 9780838937839 (paperback) | ISBN 9780838937457 (pdf) | ISBN 9780838938256 (epub)
Subjects: LCSH: Libraries—Censorship—United States. | Intellectual freedom—United States.
Classification: LCC Z711.4 .K654 2023 (print) | LCC Z711.4 (ebook) | DDC 025.2/13—dc23/eng/20220621
LC record available at https://lccn.loc.gov/2022028169
LC ebook record available at https://lccn.loc.gov/2022028170

Cover design by Kim Hudgins. Cover images © Andrii/Adobe Stock.
Text design and composition by Karen Sheets de Gracia in the Cardea and Acumin Pro typefaces.

♾ This paper meets the requirements of ANSI/NISO Z39.48-1992 (Permanence of Paper).

Printed in the United States of America
27 26 25 24 23   5 4 3 2 1

For Aaron, with all my love.
We should get that ice cream sometime soon.

"We uphold the principles of intellectual freedom and resist all efforts to censor library resources."

—*ALA Code of Ethics* **(June 29, 2021)**

CONTENTS

Preface *ix*

Acknowledgments *xi*

1 Intellectual Freedom: A Core and Contested Value *1*

2 A History of Intellectual Freedom *17*

3 Freedom of Expression *35*

4 Information Access and Censorship *53*

5 Privacy and Intellectual Freedom *69*

6 Copyright and Intellectual Freedom *83*

7 Intellectual Freedom and the Information Professions *97*

8 Current and Future Issues in Intellectual Freedom *109*

Index *121*

PREFACE

WHEN I FIRST DISCUSSED THIS BOOK with my editor, support for intellectual freedom among librarians seemed to be on the wane. There were bitter disputes—mostly online—that centered on whether or not intellectual freedom harmed underrepresented populations and was not in keeping with the values of librarianship. The world has changed since I first agreed to write this book in 2019. I could not have imagined that there would be a global pandemic, a political insurrection in the United States, or a doubling of the number of reported book challenge cases. The latter has led to a reconsideration of the position of intellectual freedom in librarianship and, I would argue, reasons for supporting intellectual freedom as a core value of the profession and a basic human right are clearer than ever.

I have taught an elective class called Intellectual Freedom and Censorship at the School of Information Sciences at the University of Illinois at Urbana-Champaign every year except one since I first joined the faculty in 2012. The course was originally sixteen weeks and was shortened to eight weeks in 2014 to encourage more students to take the elective. Since 2015 the Freedom to Read Foundation (ftrf.org) has provided support in the form of organizing guest speakers and scholarships for non-Illinois students to take the course. In its eight-week format, the course is intensive and requires students to read a lot of material in a very short time.

The course includes two assessments that were originally designed by the previous instructor, Loretta Gaffney. The first is a presentation on intellectual freedom allies that exposes students to organizations other than the American Library Association that support intellectual freedom. A second assessment asks students to write a short overview of an intellectual freedom issue. Students may choose any topic that interests them as long as it relates to the themes of the course.

The third is a role-playing portfolio on responding to a library challenge, for which students must respond in character to one of several scenarios in a variety of library settings. The portfolio consists of five parts:

1. A 1-2 page letter of response to the complainant
2. A 1-2 page letter to the library board, school board, or decision-making committee detailing the challenge and your recommendation for resolution
3. An annotated support file of 3-4 documents
4. A 3-4 page plan for community public relations and outreach
5. A 1-2 page reflection on your process for addressing this controversy

This assessment is intended to prepare students to apply what they have learned in the course when they are confronted with an intellectual freedom challenge in their working lives. The scenarios are updated regularly and often mirror current challenges that are reported in the media.

The primary purpose of *Foundations of Intellectual Freedom* is to provide a primer on this core value. It is intended to introduce intellectual freedom to librarians and other information professionals. I use the term "information professionals" throughout to indicate *all* library workers (whether degreed or not) and workers in aligned fields including archives, museums, information sciences, and others. The book is also intended to be accessible to readers outside of information fields. Although the geographic context for the book is the United States, each chapter includes at least a brief overview of global implications of the various subjects that are presented.

The book is a distillation of the eight-week University of Illinois course. Although the emphasis and timing for any particular topic change from year to year, the subjects of the chapters in this volume form the general outline of the syllabus.

Chapter 1 introduces and defines important concepts related to intellectual freedom, including censorship, and discusses intellectual freedom as a value and a right. Chapter 2 provides an overview of the history of intellectual freedom as a modern value based primarily on the work of John Stuart Mill and how it was incorporated in the United Nations Universal Declaration of Human Rights. Chapter 3 provides context for understanding the right to freedom of expression and its intersections with free speech, hate speech, and the embeddedness of communication. Information access and censorship are the focus of chapter 4. Chapter 5 addresses privacy and intellectual freedom with an emphasis on power and context. Chapter 6 is an introduction to copyright and its impact on intellectual freedom. Chapter 7 examines the history of intellectual freedom as a core value in librarianship. Chapter 8 provides short summaries of emerging topics in intellectual freedom.

Each of the first seven chapters includes discussion questions and a list of recommended readings with short annotations. Readers should also consult the reference list at the end of each chapter for additional readings and resources. Newsworthy events, statistics, and citations are accurate as of March 2022. The book can be read as a whole or as individual chapters. The book's goal is for the reader to develop a better understanding of why intellectual freedom matters and how supporting this right leads to a more just world.

ACKNOWLEDGMENTS

THIS BOOK IS TWO YEARS LATE due to many factors and never would have been finished without the support of my community. After working as an interim associate dean for two years during the pandemic, I was able to relinquish the role with the support of my colleagues and finish this manuscript. My editor, Rachel Chance, was extremely patient over the two years of delays. My friends in Champaign, Illinois, and around the world never lost their faith in me. My parents, Jo Emily and Nathaniel Knox, have always provided love and support. Finally, my fiancé, Aaron Wilson, always had an ear for talking through the manuscript and supported me through the inevitable difficult times of writing a book.

CHAPTER 1

Intellectual Freedom

A Core and Contested Value

INTELLECTUAL FREEDOM: DEFINITIONS

"Intellectual freedom" is a term that most people have heard and yet may have only a vague sense of its definition. In the United States, for example, people often use the term "free speech" as a catchall for concepts relating to how information circulates instead of using intellectual freedom. There are some who might say that intellectual freedom has something to do with reading banned books or writing offensive content on Twitter. Others seem to have a sense that intellectual freedom is both important and contested but difficult to define. In her article on legal foundations for intellectual freedom, Shannon Oltmann (2016) notes that there are generally three different theoretical grounds for understanding intellectual freedom: the marketplace of ideas, democratic ideals, and individual autonomy. Each of these provides differently nuanced definitions and applications of the principle that will be discussed throughout this chapter and the book.

As noted in the introductory chapter of the tenth edition of the *Intellectual Freedom Manual* (IFM), intellectual freedom has never been officially defined by the American Library Association (ALA) even though intellectual freedom is a core value of librarianship (Jones and LaRue 2021, 3). The IFM, which is published by ALA's Office for Intellectual Freedom (OIF), offers a short definition: intellectual freedom is "the right of every individual to both seek and receive information from all points of view without restriction" (Jones and LaRue 2021, 3). Not surprisingly, this definition focuses on works which are fixed—such as books, magazines, movies, CDs, and digital files—that might be included in library collections. The meaning of free speech and freedom of expression are implied but not explicitly stated in this definition.

However, intellectual freedom does not have to be solely focused on fixed works that can be collected in a library or assigned as schoolwork. OIF itself offers a broader definition on its question-and-answer web page. Here OIF defines intellectual freedom as "the right of every individual to both seek and receive information from all points of view without restriction. It provides for free access to all expressions of ideas through which any and all sides of a question, cause or movement may be explored" (ALA n.d.). This definition includes both the circulation of works (broadly defined) and the expression of ideas.

Other definitions, like Eliza Dresang's, also explicitly include the right of the individual to have their own expression. Dresang (2006, 169) defines intellectual freedom as the "freedom to think or believe what one will, freedom to express one's thoughts and beliefs in unrestricted manners and means, and freedom to access information and ideas regardless of the content or viewpoints of the author(s), or the age, background, or beliefs of the receiver." In a previous work, *Book Banning in 21st-Century America,* I stated that intellectual freedom is "the right to access the whole of the information universe without fear of reprisal from the powers that be" (Knox 2015, 11). Outside of library and information science, the ethicist Piers Benn (2021, 2), for example, defines intellectual freedom as a state that "fosters the ability to think, speak and act without being stifled by an atmosphere of taboo, whether this is legally, intuitively, or socially enforced." This definition includes the idea that intellectual freedom is related to both explicit and implicit bans on certain ideas or knowledge.

Each of these definitions provides a window into why intellectual freedom can be difficult to define. Intellectual freedom is a condition of being—one in which an individual's mind has ultimate liberty—that is in many ways an impossible state to achieve given that, as Sue Curry Jansen (1988, 4) notes, censorship is "an enduring feature of all human communities." Individuals live in societies that each have their own norms, values, and laws, which means that intellectual freedom is always subject to circumscription. This is why it is imperative to be aware of both context and power when discussing intellectual freedom.

Throughout this book, intellectual freedom is defined as the right of every individual to hold and express opinions, and seek, access, receive, and impart information ideas without restriction. This definition is based on Article 19 of the United Nations Universal Declaration of Human Rights (1948), which states: "Everyone has the right to freedom of opinion and expression; the right includes freedom to hold opinions without interference and to seek, receive and impart information and ideas through any media regardless of frontiers." The definition used in this book explicitly includes the term "access," as this is in keeping with the core values of librarianship. The definition also refers to all aspects of the communications circuit (Darnton 1991). Article 19 is one of thirty rights and freedoms enumerated in the Universal Declaration of Human Rights, which was ratified by the United Nations in 1948. It is no mistake that in the ruins of a horrifying world war that was the deadliest in history, the United Nations included the right to freedom of opinion and expression in this document.

> **ARTICLE 19 (article19.org)**
>
> The international human rights organization ARTICLE 19 takes its name from the United Nations Universal Declaration of Human Rights. Founded in 1987, the organization bases its work on two interlocking freedoms: the freedom to speak and the freedom to know.

FLOURISHING, AUTONOMY, AND HUMAN RIGHTS

In the early twenty-first century, discussions of intellectual freedom can become heated quickly. There is no longer a general liberal consensus on the issue as there was in the mid- to late-twentieth century. One reason why discussions of intellectual freedom are so contested is that they are entangled with human rights, individual autonomy, and personal flourishing. Here "flourishing" is used as a less self-oriented term for self-actualization. As John Burgess (2016, 134) notes:

> [Flourishing] is the good that results from living in accord with the virtues. In its simplest form, flourishing is the idea that to be good is to fulfill one's purpose in life. Put another way, to flourish is to pursue the ideal self. Since everyone determines his or her ideal self, flourishing is an internally created good.

Along with classical virtues such as courage or patience, virtues can also include such concepts as caring for others or compassion for those less fortunate than oneself. This means that flourishing does not have to be solely focused on the self but can also point to whether or not others in society are flourishing. The second concept, individual autonomy, is linked to flourishing, and as Audrey Barbakoff (2010) writes, "it is not total independence, but rather the ability of an individual to make life choices guided by his or her own values." Making choices is key to both autonomy and flourishing. These ideas are linked to intellectual freedom because it is through exposure to others' ideas and opinions that we discover their values which, in turn, help us establish our own values. We then use these values to influence society.

Along with these ethical concepts, intellectual freedom is a right endowed to every individual. Rights are moral and legal entitlements that are due to human beings. Societies have a moral and legal obligation to uphold these entitlements. One method for analyzing rights is through a typology. Information philosopher Kay Mathiesen (2012) defines several types of rights that are interconnected and demonstrate how intellectual freedom is vital to human autonomy and fulfillment. First, some rights are *primary*. These are basic, fundamental rights like food, shelter, and water. There are also *linchpin* rights, which make other rights possible. The key linchpin right for intellectual freedom is the right to communicate. Mathiesen (2015, 1312) notes that the right to communicate is slightly different from the right to information or the right to expression: "Although these three rights are closely interrelated and interdependent, they differ in whether the focus is on the rights of the speaker (expression), the rights of the receiver (information), or on the rights of both at the same time (communication)." In this book, these three rights are combined into one right called intellectual freedom. Mathiesen goes on to argue that from linchpin rights come derived rights, which often focus on specific circumstances. For example, freedom of the press is a derived right that comes from the right to communicate.

Mathiesen (2012, 14) makes a strong case for communication as a linchpin right. Without it, she argues, it is impossible for humans to even understand that they have other rights: "The ability to exercise the rights of expression and access to information promotes the realization of all other human rights." Elsewhere she goes into in more detail:

> Indeed, one could argue that, without the ability to communicate, we do not have rights at all. A right licenses a person to speak up for herself. . . . One cannot claim a right if one does not know that one has the right and one cannot claim a right if one lacks the means to express oneself. The idea of claiming in relation to rights is so important that some philosophers have argued that only those who can make claims can be rights holders. While we might want to include such beings as animals and small children within the realm of rights holders, there is still something of special dignity to adult human rights holders who can take an active role in exercising their rights. (Mathiesen 2012, 15)

This discussion may seem in the weeds, but it is important to understand why intellectual freedom is so highly contested. When someone argues, for example, that they are being censored by social media companies when their accounts are removed from private platforms, they are often using arguments that are based on a misunderstanding of what rights are and the legal status of private media platforms. Also, as John Budd notes, rights are not simply about what we *should* do but what we *must* do: "When we speak of rights we should do so with care. We are not talking about situations where certain actions should be taken, we mean something more specific and more explicitly binding" (Budd 2017, 136). Intellectual freedom is at the heart of what it means to be human and a part of a community.

Many also argue that intellectual freedom is the heart of democratic society. Free inquiry is necessary to have an informed citizenry that will shape their government. Paul Sturges (2016, 169) notes:

> At its simplest, democracy is the idea that power resides in the people whose will is consulted through elections. The basic simplicity becomes more complex the closer one examines the principle and processes, but it is important to hang on to the idea that those who vote are being asked to exercise intellectual freedom. Intellectual freedom begets and supports democracy, and democracy in turn provides appropriate conditions for the further development of intellectual freedom.

The relationship between democracy and intellectual freedom can be fraught as there is always concern that free inquiry will not necessarily lead to votes and subsequent adoption of policies that will benefit all. However, this possibility becomes even more improbable without intellectual freedom.

This argument also helps to explain why intellectual freedom is necessary for social justice. Although we are all entitled to rights, they are often circumscribed by laws. In order to ensure that we are given the rights due to each of us, we must know what they are, and these rights must be claimed. This happens through communication. Having access to information and utilizing the right to intellectual freedom mean that individuals can learn about their own rights without fear of repercussions from those in power who want to deny them those rights. Freedom of expression means that they can express their knowledge of their rights to others. Although these rights are also held by those in power, upholding intellectual freedom means that people who are not part of the dominant culture have the same rights as those who are. Everyone, regardless of their social status, has the right to intellectual freedom.

CENSORSHIP

"Censorship" is the inverse of intellectual freedom. It is also a more common term that people use when they discuss issues of information access and circulation. Although in many respects all language is political, "censorship" has a decidedly more political valence than intellectual freedom. What counts as censorship often depends on both one's worldview and what one might be trying to accomplish. To employ Sue Curry Jansen's (1988) term, censorship is the knot that combines power and knowledge. Researching and analyzing censorship also provide a window into how the right to intellectual freedom is exercised in a given society.

In a previous work, I have noted that there are both broad and narrow definitions of censorship (Knox 2014b). Narrow definitions tend to focus on government censorship, while broad definitions focus on individuals or institutions. These definitions are not static and can be held by the same person or group of people at the same time. In addition, the definitions are often focused on who or what is engaging in censorship. For example, the *Intellectual Freedom Manual* defines censorship as "a decision made by a governing authority or its representative(s) to suppress, exclude, expurgate, remove, or restrict public access to a library resource based on a person or group's disapproval of its content or its author/creator" (Garnar et al. 2021, 295). This definition has a few features that should be noted. First, it focuses on the government. Second, it covers a wide range of censorship practices. Finally, it is focused on library resources. In practice, librarianship often takes a much wider view of who can engage in censorship and its effects.

The American Civil Liberties Union's (https://www.aclu.org/other/what-censorship) definition of censorship states that:

> Censorship, the suppression of words, images, or ideas that are "offensive," happens whenever some people succeed in imposing their personal political or moral values on others. Censorship can be carried out by the government as well as private pressure groups. Censorship by the government is unconstitutional.

This definition, unlike ALA's definition, includes private pressure groups as actors along with the government. It also focuses on "moral disapproval" rather than just simply "disapproval," implying that it is focused on values and ethics. Finally, its scope is wide-ranging and broader than libraries.

The dictionary definition of "censorship" refers to the transitive verb "censor" which, according to Merriam-Webster, means to "examine in order to suppress or delete anything considered objectionable" or "to suppress or delete as objectionable" (https://www.merriam-webster.com/dictionary/censor). This definition has a somewhat limited view of censorship practices and leans heavily on the word "objectionable."

In my own work, I have previously defined censorship as control over the production of texts and other cultural goods (Knox 2015, 4). This may seem overly broad, but it does capture more fully how the term is used by the general public, where it seems to mean that "someone in power has taken away my ability to circulate the knowledge that I want to in the way that I want to." The latter part is key to understanding this colloquial understanding of censorship—who has control over a particular medium is often what matters more than just what is being communicated. (This topic will be explored more in chapter 3.)

Censorship can be understood as a constellation of practices rather than a dichotomous act. Although the term is often employed this way, the question of whether or not a work or a person has been censored is rarely black and white. One way to think about censorship is to consider how someone or an entity has engaged in censorship. Jansen (1998), for example, discusses constitutive and regulative censorship. Regulative censorship refers to the type of censorship that institutions engage in and generally concerns access to information. Constitutive censorship, on the other hand, is how "the powerful invoke censorship to create, secure, and maintain their control over the power to name" (Jansen 1998, 8).

Another way to think about censorship is to consider that there are both active and passive censorship practices. Passive practices take place before a work is circulated or obtained and include self-censorship and professional bias (e.g., in acquisition practices). Active practices occur when a work is already in circulation; they include the 4 Rs:

redaction, restriction, relocation, and removal. Briefly, redaction means marking through text or images so that it cannot be viewed. Restriction and relocation are both based on whether or not a work is available to its intended audience. Restriction means that the work is, for example, put behind a desk so that someone can only access it with permission. Relocation means that the work is moved from its proper classification to another. For example, a book intended for juveniles in a library is moved to the young adult or adult section. Removal is what most people think of as censorship—a work is removed from circulation by some entity. Being aware of the level of analysis is always important for understanding censorship—engaging in censorship practices in a school district is different from engaging in censorship practices through the use of a national firewall. Both are types of censorship, but their effects are different.

> **The 4 Rs of Censorship Practices**
> - Redaction
> - Restriction
> - Relocation
> - Removal

Note that the word "work" is used above in a general sense to refer to any type of expression—not necessarily only those that are fixed, such as a book. For example, permission for protests is often restricted to certain times of day or limited to certain spaces. This might be the case for many reasons, including the safety of the participants, but these restrictions can also be understood as a censorship practice.

As with many things in life, censorship is often in the eye of the beholder. This is because censorship is inherently political and social. It is through the censorship and circulation of ideas, information, and knowledge that individuals and societies come to agreed values and norms. What is permitted to circulate and what is not defines what matters. Intellectual freedom, on the other hand, is more concretely about individuals and their personal right to information.

SOCIAL JUSTICE

Throughout this book, I argue that intellectual freedom is necessary for a just society. I acknowledge that this is a contested position and, in the early twenty-first century, many believe that social justice is not compatible with intellectual freedom. As Shannon Oltmann, Toni Samek, and Louise Cooke (2022, 8) note in the context of librarianship:

> It is fair to say that intellectual freedom is under siege from across the political spectrum, as librarians' professional and personal ethics diverge. There is a certain proportion of librarians who do not adhere to the promises of the IFLA Statement, thereby creating an ethical void and, arguably, although with positive intentions, committing a disservice to their patrons.

Although this is a longstanding argument, especially in librarianship, this critique is probably most easily viewed through the lens of the critical librarianship movement.

Critical librarianship originally began in 2014 as an extended Twitter conversation on how librarianship can more fully incorporate progressive values into practice. Critlib.org writes on their home page (http://critlib.org/about/) that the movement is "dedicated to bringing social justice principles into our work in libraries." Social justice is not fully defined by the movement but refers to bringing down the "regimes of white supremacy, capitalism, and a range of structural inequalities." Over the next few years, this movement grew online and also has sponsored several events. The hashtag #critlib is regularly used in online discussions.

In the introduction to *Knowledge Justice: Disrupting Library and Information Studies through Critical Race Theory*, Sofia Leung and Jorge López-McKnight (2021, 16) argue that critical librarianship alone is not enough and library and information science should fully incorporate critical race theory (CRT) into its theory and praxis. As they note, "CRT rejects liberal frameworks as they do not examine and center critiques of power, race, and racism. We argue that current and past diversity frameworks continue to ignore these critiques." Although intellectual freedom is not explicitly addressed in their book, the opening chapter critiques the concept of neutrality and how it is commonly used to support content-neutral policies in libraries rather than one that uplifts marginalized voices (Chiu, Ettarh, and Ferretti 2021).

Social justice, when employed as a critique of intellectual freedom, refers to the harm that an individual might endure when exposed to ideas that are hateful, biased, or discriminatory. I have written elsewhere that this perceived incompatibility is due to intellectual freedom and social justice having political foundations that are shared but with different emphases (Knox 2020). This difference can be glossed as "intellectual freedom is a liberal value while social justice is a progressive value" (Shockey 2016). However, both social justice and intellectual freedom are politically liberal orientations toward society as opposed to anarchist or conservative.

An extended Twitter discussion in January 2020 using the hashtag #timetotalk-aboutIF (https://twitter.com/talkaboutif?lang=en) provides a useful overview of some of the current discourse regarding intellectual freedom and social justice. One question that was explored was: "The current approach to IF undermines human rights b/c it acts like IF is in a vacuum—like it's, as a value, no way connected to, or reflective of, actual social and material power relations." Overall, I would argue that the progressive critique of intellectual freedom is incomplete because it does not account for power imbalances as they currently exist. That is, because we live in a world built on white supremacy, racism, heterosexism, misogyny, transphobia, ableism, and other inequities, laws and practices that are enacted to withhold information from certain groups often end up benefitting the group in power. For example, during the Black Lives Matter (BLM) protests in summer 2021, President Trump called the movement a "symbol of hate" (Sprunt and Snell 2020). If he had been empowered to censor "hate speech," Trump would never have targeted the Proud Boys in Richmond, Virginia. He preferred to (and often did) set his sights on the BLM protests that happened across the United States in the wake of George Floyd's murder.

Although strides have been made, the upheavals of recent history indicate that there is still a long way to go to a just society. In the United States, in particular, people do not have shared understandings of what constitutes hate across political and social boundaries. As with censorship, bias, prejudice, and discrimination are often, unfortunately, in the eye of the beholder.

A SOCIOLOGY OF KNOWLEDGE

Many books on intellectual freedom and, more specifically, freedom of expression, focus on the legal aspects of these concepts. Although it is important to be familiar with the law, this book is less rooted in legal frameworks for understanding intellectual freedom and is instead focused on a sociology of knowledge. Briefly, academics in this field center their work on investigating how language is "created" to make the world "real" and then to communicate that world to our fellow human beings. Communication is based in language and this area of sociology explores how knowledge is transmitted and maintained across time and space. Although an in-depth review of these theories is not necessary, it is helpful to understand what is happening when, for example, people engage in what seems to be an irrational act, such as trying to remove a database aggregator from libraries across an entire state (Cortez 2018). What are these people trying to accomplish? The theories of sociology of knowledge demonstrate that they are trying to maintain a particular reality or worldview. The resources in those databases contain not simply information but knowledge that threatens who they are as people.

In a *Social History of Knowledge* (2000), Peter Burke explores epistemic history from 1450 to the end of the eighteenth century. This time period is important because it saw the invention of the printing press by Johannes Gutenberg around 1440 (this was some time after the development of movable type in China in the eleventh century), which allowed for faster and often more reliable circulation of texts. For information professionals, one of the most important theories of the sociology of knowledge is the classification of knowledge into different types.

These types are divided into pairs and they can be useful for librarians and information professionals who are attempting to understand the arguments people are using when they attempt to restrict access to information resources. According to Burke (2000, 83), the pairs are:

1. Theoretical versus practical
2. High versus low
3. Liberal versus useful
4. Specialized versus universal
5. Public versus private
6. Legitimate versus forbidden

One approach to thinking about this is to consider the many challenges that are brought against sexual education books for children and young adults. For challengers, these books contain knowledge that should be forbidden to children even when the books are written at an appropriate age and reading level. Some people believe that sexual knowledge is only legitimate knowledge for adults. When an Arizona senator called for Robie Harris's book *It's Perfectly Normal* to be removed in December 2019, a commenter on the senator's Facebook post stated:

> Thanks for taking up the cause, but give me one good reason why "sex" needs to be added to reading, writing, and arithmetic curriculum. Schools have no legitimate cause for indoctrinating our children on matters of sex or morality; which belongs squarely on the shoulders of their parents. (https://www.facebook.com/TownsendForHouse/photos/a.10152486902763914/10157926730488914/?type=3&theater)

This comment demonstrates that intellectual freedom is truly a social and not merely political or legal phenomenon. According to the poster, schools, which are institutions that help mold future generations, should focus only on what the poster considers to be legitimate

Constructing Reality through Language

Berger and Luckmann's *The Social Construction of Reality* (1966) is a seminal work in understanding how knowledge is transmitted and maintained across generations. The authors argue that the foundations of knowledge in everyday life are based in language. Although their argument is somewhat esoteric, they are basically saying that language makes objects real. What is most important for understanding why this matters for intellectual freedom is that eventually language leads to an understanding of what is "legitimate" in a particular setting—including what knowledge is legitimate. In this typology classifying a particular knowledge as forbidden or private helps keep chaos at bay in one's life.

Language is very important for understanding censorship practices. The words that book challengers use (e.g., inappropriate, innocence, indoctrinate) are important for understanding what they are attempting to accomplish.

---

knowledge: reading writing, and arithmetic. "Sex," on the other hand, is in the realm of private and forbidden knowledge.

In her work on children and knowledge, Kerry H. Robinson (2013) argues that many censorship efforts are in relation to what she calls "difficult knowledge." This is knowledge that is linked to powerful emotional responses in adults and therefore there are often attempts to shelter children from such knowledge. This is similar to private or forbidden knowledge. Robinson argues that these attempts are often harmful because they deny children both agency and the vocabulary to describe their own bodies and lives.

This is important because it demonstrates why legal arguments are often unpersuasive in censorship cases. As will be seen throughout this book, intellectual freedom is not simply a legal construct but a social one, and the arguments that people use against the right to intellectual freedom are often social and political.

AREAS OF INTELLECTUAL FREEDOM

Intellectual freedom encompasses several interrelated areas which will be discussed throughout the chapters that follow. Although all of the areas do not map directly onto the chapters, each of the areas provides a lens through which the reader may analyze the subjects discussed in the chapters. Note that there is no hierarchical relationship between these issues—in fact, all of them are interrelated. One of the reasons why it can be difficult to research or analyze intellectual freedom is that arguments for or against intellectual freedom tend to highlight one particular theoretical or philosophical lens. For example, the idea that "information wants to be free" can be understood through the lenses of access, philosophy, policy development, and privacy.

In general, there are five areas that most scholars and practitioners focus on: access, philosophy, policy development, legal issues, and privacy. As with all typologies, these areas have a great deal of overlap (e.g., is copyright a legal issue or policy?), but it is helpful to use these areas to think through what the underlying assumptions of an argument might be. For example, when a person argues that someone should be blocked on social media or that a book should be removed from a classroom, they are making a moral and therefore philosophical argument. The response will often be a legal argument: "that's against the First Amendment" or "the Supreme Court ruled that you can't do that." These arguments are not employing the same lens for analysis and that is why people are often talking past each other when discussing intellectual freedom.

The first area, access, refers to whether or not people are able to obtain information. It can be argued that the most salient area of research for intellectual freedom is access and the defense of free inquiry. This incorporates more than just the concept of "what is on the shelf." Access includes questions of selection (what was not chosen for the shelf) and classification (how the bookshelf is arranged). Challenges to materials in libraries also fall under this umbrella because such actions threaten access. Peter Lor and Johannes Britz (2007) argue that access is a social justice issue and state that knowledge societies cannot exist without freedom of access to information. The authors use their own country, South Africa, as an example in order to demonstrate how lack of access to information can have deleterious effects on a society. "Our experience in South Africa during the apartheid years," the authors write, "taught us that restrictions on access can cause a regime to lose touch with reality. Curtailment of freedom of information is invariably associated with the dissemination of disinformation" (Lor and Britz 2007, 394). Lor and Britz describe four pillars of information societies—information and communication technology infrastructure, usable content, human intellectual capacity, and physical delivery infrastructure—which cannot be brought to fruition without access to information.

As mentioned above, Lor and Britz's thesis is heavily dependent on the concept of social justice. This links access to the next area of research issue—philosophy. One's beliefs and actions regarding intellectual freedom and censorship often rely on philosophical ideas relating to ethics, values, and morality. As an example, Lor and Britz (2007) use philosopher John Rawls's theory of justice and their own experiences in apartheid South Africa to support their view that knowledge societies must have freedom of access to information.

In *Fundamentals of Information Studies*, June Lester and Wallace C. Koehler (2007) define morals as a "set of mores, customs, and traditions that may be derived from social practice or from religious guidance." Values, in turn, are "enduring beliefs that a specific mode of conduct or end-state of existence is personally or socially preferable. Value systems are an enduring organization of beliefs" (Lester and Koehler 2007, 253). Ethics, on the other hand, are the application of values along with an area of study in philosophy.

Eliza Dresang (2006) uses "professional philosophy" as an umbrella term for the many policies and codes that librarians have developed in the area of intellectual freedom. Elsewhere, I have used the term "practical philosophy" (Knox 2014a). These terms are meant to undergird the idea that these policies are not necessarily subject to formal philosophical analysis but are often general guidelines for practice in information institutions.

These policies are part of the third interlocking issue within intellectual freedom, policy. Susan K. Burke (2008) divides these into two types: first, foundational documents, which include the IFLA Statement on Libraries and Intellectual Freedom and the ALA Library Bill of Rights, the Freedom to Read Statement, and the Freedom to View Statement that ALA developed in concert with the American Book Publishers Council. The second type of policy includes newer statements such as ALA's Code of Ethics and Core Values Statement. Policy development is an important interlocking issue within intellectual freedom and librarianship because it affects each librarian individually. Even if a particular librarian or other information professional does not hold to the Code of Ethics, this becomes an active choice because she or he is introduced to these statements through the professionalization process of library education.

Although in the United States these policies borrow language from the United States Constitution, First Amendment issues constitute a separate, supplementary issue within intellectual freedom. The library and legal professions in the United States hold that the right of freedom of access is guaranteed in the First Amendment of the Bill of Rights. To ensure this right is unabridged, the Freedom to Read Foundation is the legal arm of ALA that supports intellectual freedom in the courts. On a global level, Article 19 of the Universal Declaration of Human Rights focuses on freedom of expression (UN 1948). This indicates that members of the global community have recognized freedom of access to be a legal and moral right of humanity. The IFLA Statement on Libraries and Intellectual Freedom mirrors much of the language found in Article 19.

The final interlocking issue within intellectual freedom and censorship is closely related to the legal realm and involves issues of privacy. Within librarianship, the most common privacy issues are internet filtering and records management. There are many research articles that discuss the Children's Internet Protection Act (CIPA) and the effect of the PATRIOT Act on libraries in the United States. However, government censorship of the internet is a global issue. In their article on censorship and internet search engines, Mark Meiss and Filippo Menczer (2008) compare search results in different coutries. Because "search engines are essential in discovering new sources of information . . . a censored search engine can hide that a blocked site even exists. How can you know what you're not being shown?" As with issues of selection, "what is not on the shelf" is just as important as "what is on the shelf." Although Meiss and Menczer's article primarily describes the search comparison tool, using the interface allows users to viscerally experience how censorship impedes access to information.

BOOK OVERVIEW

Some might argue that the social ills of the early twenty-first century have shown us the negative consequences of what unfettered access to information can do. Writing this in the midst of the coronavirus pandemic means that we are inundated with false information concerning the spread of SARS-CoV-2 and the efficacy of the vaccinations that will save lives. Challenging political situations around the world are exacerbated by the ubiquity of misinformation and disinformation on the web, in addition to the inciting language that is used to encourage people to attack political and society enemies.

This book is not intended to answer all of the questions raised by these issues but to provide a framework for understanding what intellectual freedom is and why it is an important value for not only librarians and other information professionals, but also to ensure that the entire world is able to meet the challenges of the information age. As noted above, although this book will discuss the legal aspects of intellectual freedom and censorship, that is not its focus. Instead, the book will discuss these ideas as social phenomenons based in frameworks of the circulation of knowledge, print and digital cultures, and reading practices. That is, the book argues that how a society views intellectual freedom and censorship is based on how knowledge is understood to be absorbed and acted upon by individuals. Legal frameworks such as the First Amendment law in the United States and hate speech laws in the European Union are just one aspect of the overall foundation for discussions in the book.

Note that in the preceding paragraph, the subject of the book was listed as "intellectual freedom and censorship." This is because it is difficult to discuss one without the other. In many ways, intellectual freedom is the opposite of censorship. However, I hope to demonstrate in the following chapters that intellectual freedom is much broader and richer than simply allowing or denying access to information. Intellectual freedom is vital to thriving both as an individual and as a society. Censorship, on the other hand, is a group of negative practices that are often based on fear of the unknown.

Intellectual freedom is also intimately tied to ideas of social justice. Social justice has many meanings but, when it comes to knowledge, social justice centers on basic questions of what, who, and how. What types of knowledge should be out of bounds? Who makes those decisions? How is that knowledge circulated in society? The answers to these questions are disputed in the early twenty-first century. Western societies are grappling with their white supremacist, colonialist, heteronormative, ableist, and classist histories sometimes in ways that seem at odds with the value of intellectual freedom.

I, and therefore this book, take the position that social justice is impossible without intellectual freedom. It is only through the free circulation of ideas that citizens can understand what the terms "white supremacist," "colonialist," "heteronormative," "ableist," and "classist" even mean. It is in the interest of those in power to not allow these ideas to become part of everyday parlance. Throughout this book, I hope to show that censorship only helps those in power. I fully recognize that some readers will not be convinced; however, I hope that the book at the very least explains why arguments advocating censorship of hateful and hurtful ideas are not always the best course of action when attempting to protect the voices of people who are marginalized.

Some caveats are in order. This book is not meant to be a comprehensive overview of all intellectual freedom issues, and there will inevitably be some information that is left out or glossed over. Readers are encouraged to explore the supplementary readings listed at the end of each chapter. In addition, this book is primarily focused on intellectual freedom in the United States, although there is some discussion of intellectual freedom issues around the globe. Finally, although the primary audience for the book is all library workers and other information professionals, it is intended to be accessible and of interest to all who want to know more about intellectual freedom. Readers may consider reading this primer in tandem with the latest edition (at the time of this writing, the tenth edition) of the *Intellectual Freedom Manual* (2021) in order to have practical guidelines and parameters for better understanding intellectual freedom as a fundamental value of librarianship and related fields.

This introductory chapter sets the stage for exploring several aspects of intellectual freedom. The rest of the book is divided into seven areas that provide breadth in understanding the issues that constitute intellectual freedom. None is meant to be exhaustive, and the reader is again encouraged to explore the supplementary bibliographies at the end of each chapter.

Chapter 2 focuses on the historical foundations of intellectual freedom. It includes discussion of John Stuart Mill's *On Liberty*, US court cases, and some information about IFLA and the Committee on Freedom of Access to Information and Freedom of Expression (FAIFE) and provides historical, philosophical, and legal overviews of the topic. Chapter 3 discusses the value of freedom of expression and includes an overview of current issues such as protection for hate speech in the United States as well as misinformation and disinformation. Chapter 4 centers on information access and provides an overview of what access means as well as other issues such as internet filtering, pro- and anti-censorship arguments, and a short discussion of book banning. Privacy is the focus of chapter 5. It is primarily concerned with definitions of privacy and its relationship to information services. Chapter 6 is on copyright and provides a brief overview of US copyright law with a focus on fair use as well as some discussion of international copyright law. Chapter 7 discusses how intellectual freedom is supported within the information professions. Finally, the book concludes with a chapter that explores current and future issues in intellectual freedom.

It should be clear that intellectual freedom has two dominant concepts: information access and freedom of expression. These work in tandem with each other because one leads to the other: there is no information to access without the freedom of expression, which leads to there being information for people to access. This is clearly part of the communications circuit (Darnton 1991). It is hoped that this book will provide a foundation for understanding why supporting intellectual freedom is an important professional and personal value to hold in the information age.

DISCUSSION QUESTIONS

- How do you define intellectual freedom? Censorship? Social justice?
- Have you encountered censorship practices in your own life? Personal or professional?
- Do you agree that intellectual freedom is necessary for social justice? Why or why not?
- What does it mean to flourish as a human being? As a society?

FURTHER READING

Alfino, Mark, and Laura Koltutsky, eds. 2014. *The Library Juice Press Handbook of Intellectual Freedom: Concepts, Cases, and Theories.* Sacramento, CA: Library Juice Press.
   This volume of essays covers the gamut of intellectual freedom issues from theoretical foundations to specific areas, including journalism, defamation, and government secrecy. It is an excellent resource for understanding a wide variety of debates within intellectual freedom.

Atkins, Robert, Svetlana Mintcheva, and National Coalition against Censorship (U.S.), eds. 2006. *Censoring Culture: Contemporary Threats to Free Expression.* New York: New Press.
   The authors of the essays in this collection provide a wide array of perspectives on censorship. Although it was published some time ago, the essays remain relevant to intellectual freedom debates today.

Benn, Piers. 2021. *Intellectual Freedom and the Culture Wars.* New York: Palgrave Macmillan.
   There are very few books outside of library and information sciences that focus on intellectual freedom, and Benn's monograph is one of the few examples. This ethical treatise provides a well-reasoned, philosophical justification for intellectual freedom.

Garnar, Martin, Trina Magi, and Office for Intellectual Freedom, eds. 2021. *Intellectual Freedom Manual.* 10th ed. Chicago: American Library Association.
   The most recent edition of the *Intellectual Freedom Manual* is a crucial resource for anyone interested in intellectual freedom and related issues. It provides clear overviews, definitions, checklists, and recommendations for implementing policies that support intellectual freedom in an information institution. Although primarily intended for library workers, it is useful for anyone interested in intellectual freedom.

Leung, Sofia Y., and Jorge R. López-McKnight, eds. 2021. *Knowledge Justice: Disrupting Library and Information Studies through Critical Race Theory.* Cambridge, MA: MIT Press.

This important book, which is available fully open access, pushes both academics and practitioners to reconsider firmly held theories and practices in the information professions. There are critiques of conventional ideas of intellectual freedom, information access, and freedom of expression that should be carefully considered by every librarian and information professional.

REFERENCES

American Library Association. n.d. "Intellectual Freedom and Censorship Q & A." www.ala.org/Template.cfm?Section=basics&Template=/ContentManagement/ContentDisplay.cfm&ContentID=60610.

Barbakoff, Audrey. 2010. "Libraries Build Autonomy: A Philosophical Perspective on the Social Role of Libraries and Librarians." *Library Philosophy and Practice,* January 2010. https://digitalcommons.unl.edu/cgi/viewcontent.cgi?article=1481&context=libphilprac.

Benn, Piers. 2021. *Intellectual Freedom and the Culture Wars.* New York: Palgrave Macmillan.

Berger, Peter L., and Thomas Luckmann. 1966. *The Social Construction of Reality.* New York: Anchor Books.

Budd, John. 2017. *Six Issues Facing Libraries Today: Critical Perspectives.* Lanham, MD: Rowman and Littlefield.

Burgess, John T. F. 2016. "Narrative Identity and Flourishing Within the Information Professions." *Journal of Information Ethics* 25 (1): 132–49.

Burke, Peter. 2000. *A Social History of Knowledge: From Gutenberg to Diderot.* Malden, MA: Polity Press.

Burke, Susan K. 2008. "Removal of Gay-Themed Materials from Public Libraries: Public Opinion Trends, 1973–2006." *Public Library Quarterly* 27 (3): 247. https://doi.org/10.1080/01616840802229552.

Chiu, Anastasia, Fobazi Ettarh, and Jennifer A. Ferretti. 2021. "Not the Shark, but the Water." In *Knowledge Justice: Disrupting Library and Information Studies through Critical Race Theory*, edited by Sofia Y. Leung and Jorge R. López-McKnight, 49–71. Cambridge, MA: MIT Press.

Cortez, Marjorie. 2018. "State School Board Supports Restoring Access to Education Database after Parent Finds Inappropriate Content." *Deseret News*, October 6, 2018. https://www.ksl.com/article/46401030/state-school-board-supports-restoring-access-to-education-database-after-parent-finds-inappropriate-content.

Darnton, Robert. 1991. "What Is the History of Books?" In *Kiss of Lamourette: Reflections in Culture,* 107–35. New York: W. W. Norton and Company.

Dresang, Eliza T. 2006. "Intellectual Freedom and Libraries: Complexity and Change in the Twenty-First-Century Digital Environment." *Library Quarterly* 76 (2): 169–92. https://doi.org/10.1086/506576.

Garnar, Martin, Trina Magi, and Office for Intellectual Freedom, eds. 2021. *Intellectual Freedom Manual.* 10th ed. Chicago: American Library Association.

Jansen, Sue Curry. 1988. *Censorship: The Knot That Binds Power and Knowledge.* New York: Oxford University Press.

Jones, Barbara M., and James LaRue. 2021. "What Is Intellectual Freedom?" In *Intellectual Freedom Manual*, edited by Martin Garnar et al., 10th ed., 3–17. Chicago: American Library Association.

Knox, Emily J. M. 2014a. "Supporting Intellectual Freedom: Symbolic Capital and Practical Philosophy in Librarianship." *Library Quarterly* 84 (1): 1–14.

———. 2014b. "The Books Will Still Be in the Library: Narrow Definitions of Censorship in the Discourse of Challengers." *Library Trends* 62 (4).

———. 2015. *Book Banning in 21st-Century America.* Beta Phi Mu Scholars. Lanham, MD: Rowman and Littlefield.

———. 2020. "Intellectual Freedom and Social Justice: Tensions Between Core Values in American Librarianship." *Open Information Science* 4 (1): 1-10. https://doi.org/10.1515/opis-2020-0001.

Lester, June, and Wallace C. Koehler. 2007. *Fundamentals of Information Studies: Understanding Information and Its Environment*. New York: Neal-Schuman Publishers.

Leung, Sofia Y., and Jorge R. López-McKnight. 2021. "Introduction: This Is Only the Beginning." In *Knowledge Justice: Disrupting Library and Information Studies through Critical Race Theory*, edited by Sofia Y. Leung and Jorge R. López-McKnight, 1-41. Cambridge, MA: MIT Press.

Lor, Peter Johan, and Johannes Jacobus Britz. 2007. "Is a Knowledge Society Possible without Freedom of Access to Information?" *Journal of Information Science* 33 (4): 387-97. https://doi.org/10.1177/0165551506075327.

Mathiesen, Kay. 2012. "The Human Right to Internet Access: A Philosophical Defense." *International Review of Information Ethics* 18 (12): 9-22.

———. 2015. "Human Rights as a Topic and Guide for LIS Research and Practice." *Journal of the Association for Information Science and Technology* 66 (7): 1305-22. https://doi.org/10.1002/asi.23293.

Meiss, Mark, and Filippo Menczer. 2008. "Visual Comparison of Search Results: A Censorship Case Study." *First Monday*, June 2008. https://doi.org/10.5210/fm.v13i7.2019.

Oltmann, Shannon M. 2016. "Intellectual Freedom and Freedom of Speech: Three Theoretical Perspectives." *Library Quarterly* 86 (2): 153-71. https://doi.org/10.1086/685402.

Oltmann, Shannon M., Toni Samek, and Louise Cooke. 2022. "Intellectual Freedom: Waving and Wavering across Three National Contexts." *IFLA Journal*, March 2022, 03400352221085294. https://doi.org/10.1177/03400352221085294.

Robinson, Kerry H. 2013. *Innocence, Knowledge, and the Construction of Childhood: The Contradictory Nature of Sexuality and Censorship in Children's Contemporary Lives*. London; New York: Routledge.

Shockey, Kyle. 2016. "Intellectual Freedom Is Not Social Justice." *Progressive Librarian*, no. 44 (Spring): 101-10.

Sprunt, Barbara, and Kelsey Snell. 2020. "Trump: Painting 'Black Lives Matter' on 5th Avenue Would Be 'Symbol Of Hate.'" *NPR*, July 1, 2020. https://www.npr.org/sections/live-updates-protests-for-racial-justice/2020/07/01/885944289/trump-painting-black-lives-matter-on-5th-avenue-would-be-symbol-of-hate.

Sturges, Paul. 2016. "Intellectual Freedom, Libraries and Democracy." *Libri* 66 (3): 167-77. https://doi.org/10.1515/libri-2016-0040.

United Nations. 1948. "The Universal Declaration of Human Rights." 1948. www.un.org/en/documents/udhr/.

CHAPTER 2

A History of Intellectual Freedom

CONTEXTUALIZING INTELLECTUAL FREEDOM

Intellectual freedom is not a term that is commonly used outside of academia, librarianship, and other closely related information professions. The general public tends to use the terms "censorship" or "free speech" when discussing the circulation of ideas and possible repercussions. These terms are often used interchangeably even though they refer to different phenomena. One example is the common assertion that social media platforms "censor free speech" by blocking users from their platforms. This statement has an extraordinary amount of history built into it and must be understood as reflecting specific ideas about human and individual rights as well as the obligations of new communications platforms.

In an article on the history of intellectual freedom, Caitlin Ratcliffe (2020, 14) notes:

> Intellectual freedom as we understand it in LIS [library and information science] was not articulated until the 1930s. Prior to that, freedom of expression (and variations thereof) were the terms used to describe the set of values that would eventually become known as intellectual freedom.

Ratcliffe argues that intellectual freedom is inherently tied to European Enlightenment values such as liberty and rational thought and to a particular conceptualization of the individual and their place in society. As will be shown, these values were eventually incorporated into the theories of Western philosophers, most importantly by nineteenth-century utilitarian John Stuart Mill.

To review additional data for the historical use of the term "intellectual freedom," enter it into Google's Ngram (https://books.google.com/ngrams), which provides an overview of when terms appear within the over forty million title corpus of Google Books for a given year. The phrase "intellectual freedom" does not appear on Google's Ngram Viewer until 1857—just prior to the publication of Mill's *On Liberty*. This is not surprising considering that the 1850s, at the early middle of Queen Victoria's reign in the United Kingdom, were a time of political stability. This was also the time of the rise of several modern philosophical traditions, including utilitarianism, of which Mill was a part.

The focus of this chapter is on the history of intellectual freedom as a personal and professional value as well as a human right. However, the history of intellectual freedom is, of course, intricately intertwined with the history of censorship. Therefore, the chapter will begin with a brief history of censorship before tracing the history of intellectual freedom as a value and a right from its origins as an Enlightenment value to its adoption by the US library community in the 1930s. This history will also touch upon some of the controversies that have arisen over time.

This chapter is titled "*a* history" rather than "*the* history" of intellectual freedom because there is not, of course, a single history of the concept. Because I am writing from the perspective of someone who lives in the United States, the history presented here is biased and centers on Western, colonialist concepts of knowledge circulation. It privileges developments in Europe and the United States over the history of intellectual freedom and censorship in Asia and the Global South. Although the chapter does discuss the adoption of intellectual freedom as a core value of librarianship for librarians around the globe in the twentieth century, it centers on European and United States history. By way of explanation, I take to heart Ralph Wiley's response that "Tolstoy is the Tolstoy of the Zulus" and Ta-Nehisi Coates's (2013) subsequent elaboration on this idea and argue that the history of intellectual freedom, although primarily discussed through the written essays of white, cis-male philosophers, is a history of a value that has been adopted throughout the world. Readers are invited to research the history of these concepts in their own nations and communities to further expand the information presented here.

A VERY BRIEF HISTORY OF CENSORSHIP

In contrast to documented histories of intellectual freedom, there are many documented histories of censorship. As with other histories of knowledge, histories of censorship tend to focus on the Global North and begin with the office of the *censor* in Rome. However, we know that censorship of written works was also practiced in China. For example, the first emperor of unified China, Qin Shi Huang, destroyed books in 213 BCE and also buried alive scholars who owned forbidden books. One also suspects that censorship was a foundational aspect of civilizations around the world because, as the cliché states, knowledge is power, and all governments have a vested interest in keeping some types of information out of the hands of the general public. There are no comprehensive histories of precolonial censorship in Africa, Asia, and South America.

To date, there is not a single, definitive volume that covers the history of world censorship. Instead, there are many different monographs or multivolume sets that give an overview of censorship practices around the world using different analytical lenses. For example, there are several encyclopedias of censorship, which consist of articles that trace censorship in particular countries or regions as well as case law and movements. The 1990 *Encyclopedia of Censorship* published by Facts on File, along with its update in 2005, states the editors' intention:

> [I] tried to tabulate as comprehensively as possible in this encyclopedia the history, development, and present-day state of the censor's art. I have taken as a model the essential catholicity of the Oxford Companions to English and to American Literature. I have concentrated, inevitably, on America and Britain, followed closely by other Western nations (including South Africa,) Europe and the communist bloc, China and the Third World. (Green and Karolides 2005, xxi)

Along with encyclopedias, there are also numerous bibliographies of censored works; in many respects, these bibliographies offer the most comprehensive documentation of censorship history. Some examples include the series of works published in 2006 by Nicholas J. Karolides, Dawn B. Sova, and Margaret Bald that were published by Facts on File. The series presents censorship histories of books in several different arrangements. One set, for example, collects summaries and censorship histories on the grounds on which the books were censored: political, religious, sexual, or social. The American Library Association publishes a yearly bibliography (called a field report) of books that have been challenged in the United States. These are then consolidated in a regular basis into a larger volume (Doyle 2017). By cataloging which works have been censored over time and the reasons why they were censored, a full picture of both the ubiquity of censorship and the changing mores and values of societies emerges.

One lens for understanding censorship is to focus on various societal structures and particular historical frameworks for suppressing knowledge. These frameworks are models for analyzing censorship practices. Models of censorship can focus on who is engaging in the practice. For example, is it the state or an individual who is doing the censoring? Or an individual using the power that a state has invested in him or her? The term "censorship" itself comes from a state-sponsored Roman title of censor, "one who monitors morality." The censor was an official office with two men appointed to the position. The censor was concerned with how male citizens fulfilled their duties, especially their *"regimen morum*: the discipline of moral practices" (Green and Karolides 2005, 95). The Roman empire ended this office in 22 BCE.

The royal privilege of early modern Europe was also a form of state-sponsored censorship.

> By granting a privilege, the king did not merely allow a book to come into being: he put his stamp of approval on it; he recommended it to his subjects, speaking through one or more censors who expatiated on its importance and even its style in long-winded permissions and approbations that were usually printed in the book along with a formal *lettre de privilège* from the king. (Darnton 1979, 27)

In *ancien régime* France, only works with the royal privilege—that is, the endorsement of the monarch—could be printed. A similar system also existed in Great Britain as the licensing acts of the seventeenth century were all forms of prepublication censorship by the state in the guise of the king. As Petley (2009, 35) notes, the effects of these acts are difficult to measure as they probably led to prior restraint among authors. John Milton's *Areopagitica* (1644) is a well-known example of a work on the environment of censorship that was produced by the Licensing Acts—as well as a defense of intellectual freedom that was published without an imprimatur. Milton argues for "promiscuous" reading and states that "truth and understanding are not such wares as to be monopolized and traded in by tickets and statutes and standards" (Milton 1644, 123). Milton (1644, 102) also provides a defense of books that is recognizable to anyone who is concerned about censorship, although it is couched in somewhat startling terms:

> And yet on the other hand unless wariness be used, as good almost kill a man as kill a good book; who kills a man kills a reasonable creature, God's image; but he who destroys a good book kills reason itself, kills the image of God, as it were in the eye.

This is a strong argument, but it speaks to the book as a technology that allows ideas to be transmitted regardless of time and space, which is one of the reasons why they are subject to censorship.

Institutional censorship is another model for analyzing censorship practices. For example, from 1559 to 1996 the Roman Catholic Church published a list of books that were considered to be heretical, impure, or obscene. Punishment for owning books listed in the *Index Liborum Prohibitorum* was excommunication (Green and Karolides 2005, 258). During pre-Enlightenment times, it listed works by Martin Luther, Galileo, and most Greek and Roman classics. Nikos Kazantzakis's *The Last Temptation of Christ,* which eventually was made into a controversial film by Martin Scorsese, was listed in 1953. The last two books to be listed were by Simone de Beauvoir: *The Second Sex* and *The Mandarins*. Like all such lists, the bibliography provides insight into the predilections of the church at any given time. It should also be noted that lines between institution and state can sometimes blur if one considers that in many countries the church was the state. The censorship practices of social media companies such as Twitter or Meta can also be classified as a form of institutional censorship.

These models of censorship are not always distinct and individuals can, for example, draw on the power of an institution or the state to engage in censorship practices. Anthony Comstock, a United States Postal Inspector in the Victorian era, is a clear example of this. Although he was one person, he used his position to bar access to materials that came through US ports. The fact that the anti-obscenity Comstock Laws bear his name is a testament to his power. Gilded Age anti-vice societies, on the other hand, were directly related to the collective influence of individuals who were part of non-governmental entities. These societies, located in New York and Boston, censored materials in library and museum collections (Beisel 1997). Censors tend to use whatever tools are available to impede access to knowledge that they deem to be harmful or dangerous.

INTELLECTUAL FREEDOM BEFORE THE NINETEENTH CENTURY

As noted, rather than focusing on the history of censorship, this chapter will focus on the history of intellectual freedom. The history of this value and right is, of course, intertwined with the concepts of knowledge circulation, freedom of expression, and censorship. It is also a history tied to the development of the concept of fundamental human rights, which are—in turn—tied to Enlightenment ideas concerning the individual and what people are owed simply because they are humans.

In her previously mentioned comprehensive essay on intellectual freedom and values, Caitlin Ratcliffe (2020, 14) argues that intellectual freedom is an Enlightenment value that is liked to the theory of personal free expression:

> Prior to the Enlightenment, the English—and the first American colonists, who theoretically enjoyed the same rights and liberties as the English under the 1606 Charter for Virginia—were guaranteed personal liberty by the Magna Carta (1215). Following the Glorious Revolution, the English Bill of Rights (1689) granted the freedom of speech in Parliament. Notably, the English Bill of Rights did not guarantee complete freedom of expression. The British Parliament restricted printers throughout the eighteenth century (Feldman, 2008) and dramatists continued to be censored until 1968 (Shellard, Nicholson, and Handley, 2004). However, thinkers such as John Locke and Voltaire

brought the Classical-era value of free speech, first articulated in a "Western" context by Socrates and Plato, to the forefront of the self-proclaimed Age of Reason.

Freedom of expression is discussed in further detail in chapter 3, but it is important to note that intellectual freedom can be understood best as an individual rather than a group right. Ratcliffe (2020) also notes that the values of free expression, as well as religious and political dissent, spread during the seventeenth and eighteenth centuries and are "foundations of modern democratic ideology." I would also argue that these are foundations of classical liberal philosophy, which eventually became one of the defining schools of political thought in the democratic West. Classifying intellectual freedom as an individual rather than a group or collective right is also salient to the discussion of how the right intersects with other rights, including social justice.

MILL, TRUTH, AND THE MARKETPLACE OF IDEAS*

As I have mentioned elsewhere, John Stuart Mill is the philosopher most strongly associated with the right to intellectual freedom (Knox 2019). Mill was born in England in 1806 and his father was a friend of Jeremy Bentham, considered to be the founder of modern utilitarianism. Mill eventually became a utilitarian philosopher and expanded on Bentham's work. Mill was greatly influenced by his partner Harriet Taylor, and there is some evidence that she helped write *On Liberty* (Miller 2019). Utilitarians are primarily associated with the idea that ethical decisions should be based on reducing harm and maximizing goods. This is a consequentialist ethical framework that holds that "the relevant consequences, in particular, are the overall happiness created for everyone affected by the action" (Stevenson n.d.). For Mill, this idea is linked to the concept of truth, which helps us know if we are making good decisions that lead to justice. What is true is what is best for the most people, but how do we discover what is true? While Bentham was primarily concerned with truth in the courtroom, Mill was concerned with the court of public opinion.

According to Alan Ryan (2011, xv), editor of the Penguin Classics edition of *On Liberty*, Mill was concerned with the effects of public opinion and, after reading Alexis de Tocqueville's *Democracy in America*, the fear of the tyranny of the majority.

> De Tocqueville wanted to discover why democracy in France brought with it revolution, dictatorship and violence, while nothing like it had happened in the United States, or in Britain. What he discovered was that the United States and Britain were threatened by a gentler form of repression. This was the tyranny of opinion that Mill wrote *On Liberty* to combat.

In Mill's understanding, truth itself is a kind of utility.

It is difficult to overstate the importance of *On Liberty* to the development of the principle of intellectual freedom. Mill's argument is based on two ideas. First, the idea that truth exists and, second, it must be discerned through rigorous debate. That is, one

---

* Thank you to John Burgess for his help with this section.

> **Act Utilitarianism, Rule Utilitarianism, and Consequentialism**
>
> At its most basic, utilitarianism calls for people to make decisions based on what will lead to the greatest happiness for the greatest number of people. Act utilitarianism focuses on actions that are good if they produce more unhappiness than unhappiness, while rule utilitarianism calls for the adoption of rules that lead to more total happiness. Utilitarianism is consequentialist and focuses on the outcomes (i.e., the consequences) of ethical decisions rather than deontological, focusing on the duties of the individual.

can only know that something is true if you hear the arguments against that truth. First published in 1859, the ideas that are presented in the essay are the philosophical foundation for the right to free expression. Mill's argument from truth consists of the following premises:

1. Silenced opinions may be true.
2. Silenced opinion may contain some grain of truth even if it is held in error.
3. Truth must be contested or it is simply prejudiced opinion.
4. The meaning of truth must be held with conviction from reason.

This argument may also be presented as a question: "How can you know if what you believe is true if you do not hear the arguments of those who disagree with you?" Mill's theory eventually led to the concept of a marketplace of ideas where the truth will win out in the end. As Nigel Warburton (2009, 25) notes, this marketplace will "increase the likelihood of achieving the best result, namely the emergence of truth and the elimination of error."

Although it has not always been the focus of analysis of Mill's theory, another important aspect is the harm principle, which states that Mill's consequentialist theory holds that protection from harm is the sole justification for interference.

> The object of this Essay is to assert one very simple principle, as entitled to govern absolutely the dealings of society with the individual in the way of compulsion and control, whether the means used be physical force in the form of legal penalties, or the moral coercion of public opinion. That principle is, that the sole end for which mankind are warranted, individually or collectively, in interfering with the liberty of action of any of their number, is self-protection. That the only purpose for which power can be rightfully exercised over any member of a civilized community, against his will, is to prevent harm to others. His own good, either physical or moral, is not a sufficient warrant. (Mill 1859, 15-16)

Mill's entire treatise and the idea of the marketplace of ideas are increasingly the targets of critique as the right to freedom of expression and intellectual freedom are contested. Mill and other philosophers of his time could not have imagined the marketplace of the internet and how easy it would be for anyone to publish and for ideas to circulate. What constitutes harm, what should be done in response to harm, and how these issues relate to the truth are all topics of robust discussion in various quarters.

Although Mill's harm principle does provide a philosophical justification to limit unfettered access to knowledge, his theory is usually not used for this purpose. The Millian metaphor, used by US Supreme Court Justice William O. Douglas following the use of a similar phrase by Justice Oliver Wendell Holmes, not only implies that ideas operate on a level playing field but also that the best "product," which in this case is truth, will come out on top.

One of the most well-known critiques is by John Rawls, who also criticized utilitarianism more generally. Rawls's theory of justice focuses on two ideas. First is the quality of assignment of rights and liberties and second, the idea that inequalities must be compensated (Rawls 2004, 59). As Robert Amdur (2009, 108) notes,

> [Rawls] seems to be making two general points. First, even if Mill has made a strong case for liberty (or for certain specific liberties), it may not be a case for equal liberty. . . . Second, and more important, the case for liberty is itself precarious, relying as it does on the result of utilitarian calculations.

Rawls's critique of Mill's theory is based on his overall critique of utilitarianism as Rawls did not feel that utilitarianism provided a sound foundation for building a just and equal society.

LIS philosopher Sam Popowich (2022, 4) states that Mill's conceptualization of intellectual freedom is overly individualistic.

> We can see in Mill all the hallmarks of the contemporary discourse of Intellectual Freedom. Individuality, reformulated as individual rights enshrined in various Constitutions; freedom as an individual possession in conflict with social or collective responsibilities; the fear of censorship as the wielding of social power by the state and the attendant defeat of individualism. These are all ways in which Intellectual Freedom is conceived within the larger structure of liberal political and legal thought.

Here Popowich argues that a collective theory of intellectual freedom is necessary to bring about a more just society.

Richard A. Parker also provides an overview of several critiques of the metaphor of the marketplace of ideas. He notes that it is linked to the modernist belief that truth not only exists but is discoverable (Parker 2009, 5). According to Parker, there are two primary critiques. First, that the marketplace is responsive to power dynamics that include "transaction costs" and second, a postmodernist critique based on the idea that there is not a priori existence of truth.

Nevertheless, Parker (2009, 8) notes that the metaphor persists:

> The value system of the marketplace of ideas metaphor is a preference for unregulated—as opposed to governmentally-restricted—speech. Supreme Court Justices use the metaphor in order to assign presumption to an unregulated communication environment. When they do this, they assign to critics of the metaphor the responsibility to explain why, at a philosophical level, governmental regulation of speech is preferable to free and open debate. Critics of the marketplace of ideas fail to address the burden of proof they inherit: to argue for the comparative superiority of a regulated arena (as opposed to an unregulated one) for public discussion.

In the years since Parker published his analysis, there have been more responses that call for a regulated public discourse. In librarianship, this often takes the form of criticism of neutrality in library philosophy. This philosophy was most clearly articulated by D. J. Foskett in his 1962 essay *The Creed of a Librarian: No Politics, No Religion, No Morals*:

> During reference service, the librarian ought virtually to vanish as an individual person, except in so far as his personality sheds light on the working of the library. He must be the reader's alter ego, immersed in his politics, his religion, his morals. He must have the ability to participate in the reader's enthusiasms and to devote himself wholly and wholeheartedly to whatever cause the reader has at the time of the enquiry. He must put himself in the reader's shoes. (Foskett 1962, 10)

In an editorial on Foskett's *Creed*, McMenemy (2007) notes that his students had started to question neutrality as a basis for librarianship in the early 2000s. More recently, Anastasia Chiu, Fobazi Ettarh, and Jennifer Ferretti (2021, 63) state that:

> A neutrally framed response holds that *all* viewpoints deserve equal weight and space in collections, when . . . authors of color are published significantly less than white counterparts. This response is underpinned by a lie—that all viewpoints are equal and valid including viewpoints that compromise the safety of People of Color [emphasis in original].

Neutrality and its related concept—the marketplace of ideas—are no longer understood as solid theoretical foundations for librarianship and other information institutions.

Along with Mill's argument from truth and a grounding in the marketplace of ideas, there are other possible philosophical justifications for intellectual freedom. For example, Ward (1990, 1986) argues:

> Deontological arguments in favor of freedom of expression, and of intellectual freedom in general, are based on claims that people are entitled to freely express their thoughts, and to receive the expressions made by others, quite independently of whether the effects of that speech are desirable or not. These entitlements take the form of rights, rights to both free expression and access to the expressions of others.

For the most part, theories of intellectual freedom should be deontological or rights-based rather than follow a consequentialist or outcomes-based philosophical foundation. In general discussion of intellectual freedom, people use both rights- and outcome-based justifications for thinking about freedom of expression and information access. However, in legal discourse, in particular, these are understood as rights that all humans have. They are also included in the United Nations Universal Declaration of Human Rights (UDHR) in Article 19. The following section discusses how intellectual freedom was understood during the development of the declaration and the context for its inclusion.

INTELLECTUAL FREEDOM AND THE UNIVERSAL DECLARATION OF HUMAN RIGHTS

It is no surprise that the Universal Declaration of Human Rights is highly responsive to the atrocities of the Nazi regime as the initial movement for the document began in 1946. The goal of both the United Nations and the declaration were articulated in Franklin D. Roosevelt's (2021) 1941 famous State of the Union speech on the four freedoms: freedom of speech, freedom of worship, freedom from want, and freedom from fear. Article 19, which incorporates three of these concepts, underwent many revisions and discussions as it was being developed.

In his comprehensive history of the Universal Declaration of Human Rights, Johannes Morsink (2010, 15) notes that the UN delegates decided on a declaration rather than a convention or covenant because a declaration is less detailed and "the parties need to agree on the principles to be proclaimed and then proclaim them . . . the truth is that nations can walk away from a declaration far more easily than from a signed covenant." There are two covenants that eventually came out of the principles enumerated in the UDHR: the International Covenant on Civil and Political Rights (ICCPR) and the International Covenant on Economic, Social and Cultural Rights (ICESCR). The drafting committee for Article 19 (then Article 16) met for the first time in June 1947. The complete minutes of all of the meetings, which are posted to the UN's Dag Hammarskjöld Library website (https://research.un.org/en/undhr/chr/1), provide insight into the various negotiations that went into crafting the language of the declaration. Political and religious fanaticism were top of mind for all committee members.

The issue of fascism and hate speech was one of the main topics of discussion among the committee members. The Soviet Union argued that the "freedom this article would give to the Nazis would undercut and threaten . . . the very right affirmed in the article; without the limiting clause, the article would be self-destructive" (Morsink 2010, 68). However, the USSR also defined fascism as a type of capitalism, making it difficult for the United States and other North Atlantic countries to vote for the Soviet Union's proposed amendments. In addition, these countries were concerned that the amendments would abridge their own laws concerning freedom of expression.

The votes themselves are fascinating and provide some insight into the political dynamics at play. Here is a typical example:

> The CHAIRMAN put to vote the words: "Everyone must be guaranteed freedom of thought."
> Those words were rejected by 23 votes to 9 with 8 abstentions.
> The CHAIRMAN put to vote the words: "and freedom to perform religious services."
> Those words were rejected by 24 votes to 9 with 8 abstentions.
> As a result of those two votes, the CHAIRMAN stated that the rest of the USSR amendment was automatically rejected. (UN 1948a)

To address the issue of hate speech, Morsink (2010, 72) argues that Article 7 of the declaration mitigates the openness of Article 19. Article 7 states: "All are equal before the law and are entitled without any discrimination to equal protection of the law. All are entitled to equal protection against any discrimination in violation of this Declaration and against any incitement to such discrimination" (UN 1948b). Article 7 does not change Article 19 and related articles, including 18 and 20, but it does enumerate equally important rights.

The UN would also develop the ICCPR in 1966 ("International Covenant on Civil and Political Rights" n.d.). This covenant outlaws "advocacy of national, religious, or racial hatred that constitutes incitement to discrimination, hostility or violence" (Article 20). The covenant currently has 173 signatories and is often cited as the basis of so-called European-style hate speech laws. The United States is a signatory but has not passed laws to conform to the ICCPR, especially regarding the state's continued use of capital punishment.

Rights theory has provided the most compelling alternative for understanding intellectual freedom as being related to the marketplace of ideas. Rather than focus on issues of truth, rights theory focuses on what each individual person is owed by their nation and society. As Kay Mathiesen (2015) argues, the right to intellectual freedom is derived from the linchpin right to communicate. Linchpin rights, like communication, make other rights possible and are different from primary rights like food, water, and shelter. However, the question of enforcement remains. For example, who or what body decides what constitutes incitement? This question of who has the power to decide is always embedded in issues of expression and intellectual freedom.

FIRST AMENDMENT LAW IN THE UNITED STATES

The right to freedom of expression and intellectual freedom are enshrined in the First Amendment of the United States Constitution. This section will focus on the legal structures of freedom of expression in the United States. Readers who are interested in international law and policy are encouraged to explore the work of the organization ARTICLE 19 and the journalism found in the magazine *Index on Censorship* (https://www.indexoncensorship.org).

Congress itself provides a history of the amendment on its website. James Madison's original draft underwent a few revisions, but the final amendment received little discussion. The constitutional annotator at the Library of Congress notes that "Debate in the House is unenlightening with regard to the meaning the Members ascribed to the speech and press clause, and there is no record of debate in the Senate" ("Freedom of Speech: Historical Background" n.d.).

The First Amendment states:

> Congress shall make no law respecting an establishment of religion, or prohibiting the free exercise thereof; or abridging the freedom of speech, or of the press; or the right of the people peaceably to assemble, and to petition the Government for a redress of grievances.

It combines not only freedom of speech but also religion, the press, and assembly, implying that the writers saw affinities among these concepts. This section of the chapter will provide brief summaries of important cases concerning freedom of expression and information access in the United States. Readers are encouraged to review the chapters in the *Intellectual Freedom Manual* (IFM; 2021) that begin with "The Law Regarding . . . ," (e.g., "The Law Regarding Copyright") to learn more about these and other cases that provide the legal foundation for intellectual freedom in the United States. It is also important to note that the First Amendment law directly applies to public rather than private institutions and agencies; however, there are nuances that readers should discuss with their institution's legal counsel. The legal summaries in the IFM also discuss First Amendment cases that were decided by the Supreme Court and provide precedent for interpreting the law.

Historically, there was not much litigation related to the First Amendment during the nineteenth century. The American Library Association's comprehensive list of court cases (https://www.ala.org/advocacy/intfreedom/censorship/courtcases) begins with a case from 1919. That case, *Schenck v. United States* (1919), brought the terms "clear and present danger" and the idea of "yelling fire in a crowded theater" into the general discourse regarding freedom of expression. Justice Oliver Wendell Holmes notes in his opinion that there are only a few circumstances, including these two, where the state has the authority to limit speech. This ruling was updated in *Brandenburg v. Ohio* (1969), which narrows "clear and present danger" to restricting speech that incites unlawful actions.

Another important case is *Martin v. City of Struthers* (1943), which focused on the right to receive information. Thelma Martin, a Jehovah's Witness, walked from door-to-door in her Ohio town distributing pamphlets. She was arrested for violating a city ordinance, but the Supreme Court found that both her and her neighbors' First Amendment rights had been violated by the ordinance. As Theresa Chmara notes, in 1965 "the court identified 'the fight to receive, the right to read and freedom of inquiry' among the rights protected by the First Amendment" in *Griswold v. Connecticut* (Chmara 2021, 54). This 1965 case, which made it legal for married couples to use contraception, is also important for establishing the right to privacy in the US Constitution. The individual right to privacy in the United States is not an explicit right but inferred through a series of constitutional amendments and precedent-setting court cases.

Tinker v. Des Moines Independent Community School District (1969) is crucial for establishing the rights of minors to freedom of expression. This case focused on three students who were expelled from school for wearing armbands to protest the Vietnam War. The court found the school district had violated the students' First Amendment rights to protest. Another important case for minors' rights is *Board of Education, Island Trees Union Free School District v. Pico* (1982, II), which focused on the difference between materials in a school library and materials that are required in school curricula.

> Our precedents have long recognized certain constitutional limits upon the power of the State to control even the curriculum and classroom. . . . But the current action does not require us to re-enter this difficult terrain. . . . For as this case is presented to us, it does not involve textbooks, or indeed any books that Island Trees students would be required to read. Respondents do not seek in this Court to impose limitations upon their school Board's discretion to prescribe the curricula of the Island Trees schools. On the contrary, the only books at issue in this case are *library* books, books that by their nature are optional rather than required reading.

This case, which was decided in 1982, found that it was against the US Constitution to remove books from the school library as this violated students' First Amendment right to receive information.

Although there were previous cases that discussed obscenity, *Miller v. California* (1972) established the obscenity test that is still in use today. Obscene materials are defined by the following criteria:

> (a) whether "the average person, applying contemporary community standards" would find the work, taken as a whole, appeals to the prurient interest, *Roth, supra*, at 354 U. S. 489, (b) whether the work depicts or describes, in a patently offensive way, sexual conduct specifically defined by the applicable state law, and (c) whether the work, taken as a whole, lacks serious literary, artistic, political, or scientific value. If a state obscenity law is thus limited, First Amendment values are adequately protected by ultimate independent appellate review of constitutional claims when necessary.

Obscenity, along with child sexual abuse images (i.e., child pornography) and fighting words (i.e., words that lead to violence), are not protected by the First Amendment.

These cases and others provide the legal framework for intellectual freedom in the United States. Librarians and other information professionals should be aware of national, state, and local laws that are in effect for their particular institutions. The intersection of these laws can be complicated, and often legal counsel is needed to ensure that policies adhere to legal standards.

INTELLECTUAL FREEDOM AND LIBRARIANSHIP

How did librarianship in particular become associated with the principle of intellectual freedom? Elsewhere, I have provided a historical genealogy of this adoption and will provide a short overview here (Knox 2014; 2017). Support for intellectual freedom as a core value slowly became part of the ethos of the growing profession of librarianship throughout the late nineteenth and early twentieth centuries. It was decidedly not part of the values of librarianship when the American Library Association was first constituted in 1876. The motto of the association, originally adopted in 1892, is "the best reading, for the largest number, at the least cost," and the term best was a guiding light for much of the profession.

For much of the late nineteenth and early twentieth centuries, librarianship was concerned with what is called the fiction question. Naturalistic fiction had become a phenomenon and was in demand from the public, but many librarians found novels to be unedifying and therefore excluded them from libraries. Reasons for this often centered on ideas about truth—an overall sense that fiction is "untrue" and not what the public should read to be educated. For many years, librarianship shifted between whether or not the posture toward patrons should be paternalistic or if they should be given full autonomy. Geller (1984) attributes the shift in attitude and adoption of the principle of intellectual freedom among librarians during the early and mid-twentieth centuries to changes in educational theory—a true education required an open shelf.

As Joyce M. Latham (2009) notes, the Chicago Public Library Board passed the first statement on intellectual freedom in the United States in 1936, followed quickly by the Des Moines Public Library policy. These policies formed the basis of the American Library Association's first Code of Ethics approved in 1939. The 1939 code included the following articles:

9. Provision should be made for as wide a range of publications and as varied a representation of viewpoints as is consistent with the policies of the library and with the funds available.
10. It is the librarian's responsibility to make the resources and services of the library known to its potential users. Impartial service should be rendered to all who are entitled to use the library.
11. It is the librarian's obligation to treat as confidential any private information obtained through contact with library patrons.
12. The librarian should try to protect library property and to inculcate in users a sense of their responsibility for its preservation. (ALA 1939)

Although the length and language of the code have changed over time, these principles are still present in the current ALA Code of Ethics.

Globally the largest international library organization, the International Federation of Library Associations and Institutions (IFLA) has long affirmed its allegiance to the UN

Universal Declaration of Human Rights. However, intellectual freedom was not explicitly addressed by the organization until 1976. A resolution regarding information circulation was put on the floor of the body in 1977 but, as Alex Byrne (2007, 55) notes:

> This resolution exposed underlying tensions since some members wished to use the term "access" but those from the Soviet Union insisted on "availability." The former implies that users can actually obtain a desired book or other resource, the latter only that it will be held somewhere, albeit on a restricted access as in the closed repositories characteristic of many Soviet era libraries.

The resolution eventually passed. IFLA formally and explicitly took on violations to Article 19 in 1993. The intellectual freedom arm of IFLA, the Committee on Freedom of Access to Information and Freedom of Expression (FAIFE), was founded in 1998.

Byrne notes that the push to support intellectual freedom is tied to broadening support for human rights:

> International acceptance of human rights, and specifically of the right to information, had reached a critical mass. This created a transnational agency of civil society which extended to the profession of librarianship, enabling its members to feel that they could and should make the commitment to the right to information and thus broaden the understanding of the profession's practice at this time. (Byrne 2007, 67)

I have argued elsewhere (2014) that librarians eventually solidified their support for intellectual freedom because of their acceptance of reader-response theory and the idea that it is not possible to know how any particular text might affect the reader.

These two ideas allow librarians to accept and enact intellectual freedom as a principle for their profession. Alessandra Seiter notes that "ALA's [intellectual freedom]-based praxis toward [equity, diversity, and inclusion] ironically rests on principles of equality rather than equity . . . presuming that everyone will benefit from the same supports regardless of their social positions of race, class, gender, sexuality, or ability" (Seiter 2020, 108). How to employ this principle to support equity as well as equality is the subject of chapter 3.

DISCUSSION QUESTIONS

- Is the marketplace of ideas a sound foundation for intellectual freedom? Rights theory? What other philosophical foundations might be effective?
- Should librarianship return to an ethic of neutrality? Why or why not?
- What does it mean for professional practice that intellectual freedom is a human right? How should this be weighed with other rights? (Consult the full text of the UDHR.)

FURTHER READING

Beisel, Nicola. 1997. *Imperiled Innocents: Anthony Comstock and Family Reproduction in Victorian America*. Princeton, NJ: Princeton University Press.
  Although this book focuses primarily on the "family values" of the Victorian Era, Beisel offers a cogent analysis of Anthony Comstock's work to censor knowledge through his role as Postal Inspector.

Boyer, Paul S. 2002. *Purity in Print: Book Censorship in America from the Gilded Age to the Computer Age*. 2nd ed. Madison, WI: University of Wisconsin Press.
  Boyer's book provides a thorough overview of book censorship. Although the book does cover the late twentieth century, its primary focus is on the 1880s through the 1930s. This is one of the most comprehensive histories of censorship in the United States.

Byrne, Alex. 2007. *The Politics of Promoting Freedom of Information and Expression in International Librarianship: The IFLA/FAIFE Project*. Lanham, MD: Scarecrow.
  Bryne's book provides a full history of IFLA's adoption of intellectual freedom and the establishment of the Advisory Committee on Freedom of Access to Information and Freedom of Expression.

Garnar, Martin, Trina Magi, and Office for Intellectual Freedom, eds. 2021. *A History of ALA Policy on Intellectual Freedom: A Supplement to the Intellectual Freedom Manual, Tenth Edition*. Chicago: American Library Association.
  This supplement to the tenth edition of the *Intellectual Freedom Manual* provides an overview of the development and approval of all of ALA's intellectual freedom guidelines and policies, including the Code of Ethics, the Freedom to Read and View Statements, and the Library Bill of Rights and its interpretations. The history of the interpretations includes an overview of controversial changes and subsequent revision of the Meeting Rooms interpretation (p. 191).

Geller, Evelyn. 1984. *Forbidden Books in American Public Libraries, 1876-1939: A Study in Cultural Change*. Westport, CT: Greenwood Press; Robbins, Louise S. 1996. *Censorship and the American Library: The American Library Association's Response to Threats to Intellectual Freedom, 1939-1969*. Westport, CT: Greenwood Press; and Samek, Toni. 2001. *Intellectual Freedom and Social Responsibility in American Librarianship: 1967-1974*. Jefferson, NC: McFarland.
  These three books offer a comprehensive history of intellectual freedom and librarianship in the United States. Reading all three together provides a deeper understanding of how intellectual freedom became a core value of the profession and how it is constantly contested by both the general public and librarians themselves.

Green, Jonathon, and Nicholas J. Karolides, eds. 2005. *Encyclopedia of Censorship*. New York: Facts on File.
  This one-volume encyclopedia is an update to the original edition published in 1990. Although this is a reference book, readers who are interested in the history of intellectual freedom will find the entries enlightening. Most importantly, it provides censorship histories for many different countries, including those outside of the Global North.

Ladenson, Elisabeth. 2013. "Censorship." In *The Book: A Global History*, edited by Michael Felix Suarez and H. R. Woudhuysen, 169-82. Oxford: Oxford University Press.
  This chapter in a one-volume book history monograph focuses on the history of censorship in the Global North.

Mill, John Stuart. 1859 [2011]. *On Liberty and the Subjection of Women*. London: Penguin Classics.
  Mill's classic treatise, published in 1859, is crucial for understanding the history of intellectual freedom. Mill's argument provides the foundation for classical liberal theory and is also freely available online.

Milton, John. 2014. *Areopagitica and Other Writings*. Edited by William Poole. New York: Penguin.
   Written in 1644, *Areopagitica* is also freely available online. It is recommended to anyone who is interested in intellectual freedom as it is one of the first full-throated expressions for the right to read in the modern era.

Robbins, Louise S. 2001. *The Dismissal of Miss Ruth Brown: Civil Rights, Censorship, and the American Library*. Norman, OK: University of Oklahoma Press.
   Robbins's book focuses on the public librarian in Bartlesville, Oklahoma, who was accused of being a communist sympathizer in the 1950s. Although the case was ostensibly about communist propaganda that was planted in the library, Robbins notes that members of the community were actually concerned about Brown's work for racial equality.

Wiegand, S. A., and Wiegand, W. A. 2007. *Books on Trial: Red Scare in the Heartland*. Norman, OK: University of Oklahoma Press.
   This is another historical work that focuses on censorship and communities. Like Robbins's book, it also centers on the presence of communist works in Oklahoma. Wiegand and Wiegand detail a local raid on a progressive bookstore and its implications.

REFERENCES

Amdur, Robert. 2009. "Rawls's Critique of On Liberty." In *Mill's On Liberty: A Critical Guide*, edited by C. L. Ten, 105-22. Cambridge Critical Guides. Cambridge: Cambridge University Press. https://doi.org/10.1017/CBO9780511575181.006.

American Library Association. 1939. Code of Ethics. https://www.ala.org/advocacy/sites/ala.org.advocacy/files/content/proethics/codeofethics/coehistory/1939code.pdf.

Bald, Margaret. 2006. *Banned Books: Literature Suppressed on Religious Grounds*. 2 Revised. New York: Facts on File.

Beisel, Nicola. 1997. *Imperiled Innocents: Anthony Comstock and Family Reproduction in Victorian America*. Princeton, NJ: Princeton University Press.

Board of Education, Island Trees Union Free School District No. 26 v. Pico by Pico. 1982. U.S. Supreme Court.

Brandenburg v. Ohio. 1969, 395 US 444. Supreme Court.

Byrne, Alex. 2007. *The Politics of Promoting Freedom of Information and Expression in International Librarianship: The IFLA/FAIFE Project*. Lanham, MD: Scarecrow.

Chiu, Anastasia, Fobazi Ettarh, and Jennifer A. Ferretti. 2021. "Not the Shark, but the Water." In *Knowledge Justice: Disrupting Library and Information Studies through Critical Race Theory*, edited by Sofia Y. Leung and Jorge R. López-McKnight, 49-71. Cambridge, MA: MIT Press.

Chmara, Theresa. 2021. "Libraries, the First Amendment, and the Public Forum Doctrine." In *Intellectual Freedom Manual*, edited by Martin Garnar et al., 10th ed., 53-75. Chicago: American Library Association.

Coates, Ta-Nehisi. 2013. "The White Man's Continent." *The Atlantic,* August 15, 2013. https://www.theatlantic.com/personal/archive/2013/08/the-white-mans-continent/278734/.

Darnton, Robert. 1979. *The Business of Enlightenment: A Publishing History of the Encyclopédie, 1775-1800*. Cambridge, MA: Belknap Press.

Doyle, Robert P. 2017. *Banned Books: Defending Our Freedom to Read*. Chicago: American Library Association.

Feldman, S. M. 2008. *Free Expression and Democracy in America: A History*. Chicago: University of Chicago Press.

Foskett, D. J. 1962. *The Creed of a Librarian: No Politics, No Religion, No Morals*. London: Library Association.

"Freedom of Speech: Historical Background. Constitution Annotated." n.d. Congress.Gov. Library of Congress. https://constitution.congress.gov/browse/essay/amdt1_2_1/.

Geller, Evelyn. 1984. *Forbidden Books in American Public Libraries, 1876-1939: A Study in Cultural Change.* Westport, CT: Greenwood Press.

Green, Jonathon, ed. 1990. *Encyclopedia of Censorship.* New York: Facts on File.

Green, Jonathon, and Nicholas J. Karolides, eds. 2005. *Encyclopedia of Censorship.* New York: Facts on File.

Griswold v. Connecticut. 1965, 381 US 479. Supreme Court.

"International Covenant on Civil and Political Rights." n.d. United Nations Human Rights Office. https://www.ohchr.org/en/instruments-mechanisms/instruments/international-covenant-civil-and-political-rights.

Karolides, Nicholas J. 2006. *Literature Suppressed on Political Grounds.* 2 Revised. New York: Facts on File.

Knox, Emily J. M. 2014. "Supporting Intellectual Freedom: Symbolic Capital and Practical Philosophy in Librarianship." *Library Quarterly* 84 (1): 1-14.

———. 2017. "Ethics." In *Reference and Information Services: An Introduction*, edited by Linda C. Smith and Melissa Autumn Wong, 27-62.

———. 2019. "Information Access." In *Foundations of Information Ethics*, edited by John T. F. Burgess and Emily J. M. Knox, 37-46. Chicago: ALA Neal Schuman.

Latham, J. M. 2009. "Wheat and Chaff: Carl Roden, Abe Korman, and the Definitions of Intellectual Freedom in the Chicago Public Library." *Libraries and the Cultural Record* 44 (3): 279-98.

Martin v. City of Struthers. 1943, 319 US 141. Supreme Court.

Mathiesen, Kay. 2015. "Human Rights as a Topic and Guide for LIS Research and Practice." *Journal of the Association for Information Science and Technology* 66 (7): 1305-22. https://doi.org/10.1002/asi.23293.

McMenemy, David. 2007. "Librarians and Ethical Neutrality: Revisiting the Creed of a Librarian." *Library Review* 56 (3): 177-81. https://doi.org/10.1108/00242530710735948.

Mill, John Stuart. 1859. *On Liberty.* http://gateway.proquest.com/openurl?ctx_ver=Z39.88-2003&xri:pqil:res_ver=0.2&res_id=xri:lion&rft_id=xri:lion:ft:pr:Z001576865:0.

Miller, Dale E. 2019. "Harriet Taylor Mill." In *The Stanford Encyclopedia of Philosophy*, edited by Edward N. Zalta, Spring 2019. Metaphysics Research Lab, Stanford University. https://plato.stanford.edu/archives/spr2019/entries/harriet-mill/.

Miller v. California. 1972, 413 US 15. Supreme Court.

Milton, John. 1644. *Areopagitica and Other Writings.* Edited by William Poole. New York: Penguin.

Morsink, Johannes. 2010. *The Universal Declaration of Human Rights: Origins, Drafting, and Intent.* https://doi.org/10.9783/9780812200416.

Parker, Richard A. 2009. "The Case of the Contentious Metaphor: The Marketplace of Ideas as Modernist Mystery." *Free Speech Yearbook* 44 (1): 1-14. https://doi.org/10.1080/08997225.2009.10556342.

Petley, Julian. 2009. *Censorship: A Beginner's Guide.* Oxford: Oneworld.

Popowich, Sam. 2022. "The Carrier Bag and Intellectual Freedom." *ERA*, February 2, 2022. https://doi.org/10.7939/r3-3pst-aa39.

"President Franklin Roosevelt's Annual Message (Four Freedoms) to Congress (1941)." 2021. National Archives. September 21, 2021. https://www.archives.gov/milestone-documents/president-franklin-roosevelts-annual-message-to-congress.

Ratcliffe, Caitlin. 2020. "Why Intellectual Freedom? Or; Your Values Are Historically Contingent." *Open Information Science* 4 (1): 11-28.

Rawls, John. 2004. "On Justice as Fairness." In *Social Justice*, edited by Matthew Clayton and Andrew Williams, 49-84. Malden, MA: Blackwell Publishing Ltd.

Ryan, Alan. 2011. "Introduction." In *On Liberty and the Subjection of Women*, by John Stuart Mill. London: Penguin Classics.

Schenck v. United States. 1919, 249 US 47. Supreme Court.

Seiter, Alessandra. 2020. "Libraries, Power, and Justice: Toward a Sociohistorically Informed Intellectual Freedom." *Progressive Librarian.* https://dash.harvard.edu/handle/1/37366973.

Sova, Dawn B. 2006. *Literature Suppressed on Sexual Grounds*. 2 Revised. New York: Facts on File.
Shellard, D., S. Nicholson, and M. Handley. 2004. *The Lord Chamberlain Regrets . . .: A History of British Theatre Censorship*. London: British Library.
Stevenson, Nathan. n.d. "Utilitarianism, Act and Rule." In *Internet Encyclopedia of Philosophy*. https://iep.utm.edu/util-a-r/.
Tinker v. Des Moines Independent Community School Dist. 1969, 393 US 503. Supreme Court.
United Nations. 1948a. Draft International Declaration Of Human Rights E/800, (Hundred Twenty-Eight Meeting, November 9, 1948, 52.)
———. 1948b. "The Universal Declaration of Human Rights." www.un.org/en/documents/udhr/.
Warburton, Nigel. 2009. *Free Speech*. Oxford: Oxford University Press.
Ward, D. V. 1990. "Philosophical Issues in Censorship and Intellectual Freedom." *Library Trends* 39 (1/2): 83-91.

CHAPTER 3

Freedom of Expression

FREEDOM OF EXPRESSION: A CONTESTED RIGHT

Freedom of expression is one of the most highly contested rights in our age of ubiquitous information. The right to hold beliefs and express them without fear of reprisal is something that many people cherish, but the nuances of this particular human right can be difficult to parse. What if one's beliefs are hurtful to other people? What if my post leads to violence? What is meant by "reprisal"? Is it the same as "consequences"?

Questions of if, how, and when expression should be limited or regulated regularly roil online. In library and information science, "free speech" itself has become a contested term. Meredith Farkas, for example, argued that free speech is "inextricable linked with physical violence" in an article in *American Libraries,* which garnered some eighty comments in one day (when many articles on the site do not have comments at all) (Farkas 2020). There are often arguments proposing that hate speech should be illegal and about how to respond to the prevalence of misinformation and disinformation online. These questions are difficult to answer because there are no shared values on these topics, not only in librarianship and other information professions but also in society as a whole.

This chapter will not provide definitive answers on what to do about hate speech or how to make people stop believing misinformation. It will provide context for understanding the individual right to freedom of expression and how it intersects with intellectual freedom. Issues of individual autonomy, self-realization, and social justice are intertwined with freedom of expression and will be discussed below. The chapter will provide some theoretical foundation for understanding why these are such difficult issues. It begins with a discussion of expression and its relation to knowledge as well as a review of different types of expression. It then provides an overview of linguistic and interpretive communities. It ends with a discussion of hate speech, harm, and some possible responses.

DOG WHISTLING ON INSTAGRAM

One of the reasons why freedom of expression is so difficult to discuss is that we are surrounded by expression at all times in the early twenty-first century, especially when we are online but also offline if one considers advertisements and billboards. The internet can be seen as one big forum where everyone who is connected has an opportunity to post about their beliefs, feelings, and activities. (How many people are reading and responding to these expressive acts is a different story.) If you are a person who is part of social media or posts to forums, you will inevitably run into problematic posts. This happened to me in September 2020 while scrolling through Instagram. An ad for a food delivery service came up that discussed food deserts in urban areas. One commenter posted: "Black women are only 3% of our population and the majority are on the taxpayers [sic] dime. Quit the virtue signaling." How does one respond to a post like this? Should one respond? When I presented this post to students in one of my classes, some of them stated that it this not true and therefore should be labeled as disinformation and deleted. Yet others saw this as a form of hate speech because it singles out a minority population and seems to denigrate them and therefore should be taken down due to this intention and its possible impact. In both cases, it is the impact as well as the intent and emotion behind this statement that make it difficult to grapple with.

I would argue that this comment is a "dog whistle," which is currently defined by Merriam-Webster as "an expression or statement that has a secondary meaning intended to be understood only by a particular group of people" (https://www.merriam-webster.com/dictionary/dog%20whistle). Dog whistles demonstrate why freedom of expression is often difficult to regulate even when it is clearly harmful. This post is intended to degrade Black women, but it is what the reader perceives as the intent behind it—not the words themselves—that is derogatory. Intent is important when it comes to the law, but it is much more difficult to navigate in society.

These dog whistles are also sometimes paired with euphemism or, as defined by Merriam-Webster, "the substitution of an agreeable or inoffensive expression for one that may offend or suggest something unpleasant." Dog whistles abound on all sides of the political spectrum but are often used to describe disagreements over ideology and interpretation is at the heart of understanding why freedom of expression is contested (On the Media 2022).

EXPRESSION, CONTEXT, AND INTERPRETATION

Article 19 of the United Nations Universal Declaration of Human Rights states *"Everyone has the right to freedom of opinion and expression;* this right includes freedom to hold opinions without interference and to seek, receive and impart information and ideas through any media and regardless of frontiers" [Emphasis mine] (UN 1948). A close reading of Article 19 reveals a subtle shift in wording. The article first states that everyone has the right to freedom of opinion and expression, then moves on to the right to hold opinions, and finally to the right to express information and ideas. Having opinions is different from expressing them, and this is where the difficultly of parsing the right to freedom of expression lies. The idea that people should have freedom of opinion and expression is, as mentioned above, highly contested. Some argue that there are some opinions that are simply beyond the pale and should not be expressed, that is, you may hold a particular opinion but you do not have the right to impart it.

It is important to note that arguments over freedom of expression and intellectual freedom are often arguments over who holds power at any given moment. The questions of who is doing the expressing and who would be able to interfere in that expression are always salient in these discussions and deserve careful analysis. Current discussions about freedom of expression are often about amplification and platforms. One model to consider is how expression fits into the communication circuit when thinking about freedom of expression. Robert Darnton's (1991) model is focused on books, but it is also helpful for considering information as a whole. Darnton places authors and publishers together at the topic of the circuit—and it is difficult to see how they could be separated from one another in some contexts—but how does this change when the author is the publisher? Or if the expression takes place on a supposedly neutral platform? What does it mean to express something if no one hears it?

The meaning of a text, written or otherwise, is never fixed and thus open to multiple meanings. People will interpret a given text differently across time, groups of people, or even within a single lifetime. As Stanley Fish (1982, 168) notes in regard to interpreting the written word, "interpretive strategies are not put into execution after reading . . . they are the shape of reading and because they are the shape of reading they give texts their shape, making them rather than, as it is usually assumed, arising from them." Groups of people who share interpretive strategies are called interpretive communities. In his book on the First Amendment, Fish (2020, 13) restates the thesis that it is the context that gives text meaning: "constraints—marked out in advance by the context—are not added to or imposed on the scene of expression; they give the scene of expression its shape." As will be discussed in more detail below, interpretive communities are vital for understanding the circulation of hate and other types of harmful speech.

It should also be noted that I am using the term "freedom of expression" rather than "free speech" in this chapter. The word "expression" covers more than just speech. It includes art, music, dance, protests, and texts of all kinds. Expression centers on people who are engaged in many types of endeavors rather than just people who are simply making arguments. On the other hand, the term "free speech" is often used as a type of polemic and quickly leads to discussions of hate speech. Finally, note that intellectual freedom is concerned with more than just speech and also covers ideas, information, and knowledge.

THE LAW

International law concerning freedom of expression varies widely. Some countries say they are dedicated to the freedom of expression but, in practice, do not uphold this right for their citizens. The discussion of the Soviet Union and its proposed amendments to Article 19 of the United Nations Universal Declaration of Human Rights are instructive on this point. As discussed in chapter 2, the Soviet Union preferred that information be "available" rather than "accessible." In many countries around the world, expression is "possible" but circumscribed by a host of laws and societal norms. It would be impossible to enumerate all freedom of expression laws here. Over the past few years, various countries' records regarding the right to freedom of expression have made headlines. For example, the protests in Hong Kong in 2019 and 2020 were brutally put down by police. Readers might consider reviewing the regular reports disseminated by various organizations that provide an overview of how freedom of expression is upheld around the globe. Every year, for example, the watchdog organization, ARTICLE 19, publishes a global expression report that takes into account both legal structures and actual practices when assigning countries to the category within their GxR metric (ARTICLE 19 2021).

In the United States, only a few types of speech (i.e., expression) are not protected: child sexual abuse material (legally known as child pornography), obscenity, and fighting words/true threats. According to Thomas Emerson (1970, 8), the theory of freedom of expression "rests upon a fundamental distinction between belief, opinion, and communication of ideas on the one hand, and different forms of conduct on the other." This separation of expression and action is fundamental to understanding how First Amendment law operates in the United States. Emerson notes that the US law allows expression while action is controlled. US hate crime law, as will be discussed in more detail below, focuses on the reason for the crime, but the crime (or action) is primary.

In their book on the reach of the First Amendment, Mark Tushnet, Alan K. Chen, and Joseph Blocher (2020, 2) discuss the difference between coverage and protection. Coverage refers to expression, which is relevant to the First Amendment, whereas protection refers to whether or not the expression can be banned. The first type of unprotected speech is material on child sexual abuse. What is legally called child pornography but is more accurately described as child sexual abuse images is determined through an objective test of whether an actual child is engaged in sexual acts in a visual medium. However, depictions of these acts in non-visual media are protected. The current law of the land is the Prosecutorial Remedies and Other Tools to End the Exploitation of Children Today Act or PROTECT Act of 2003, which was upheld by the Supreme Court in 2008.

The second type of unprotected speech, obscenity, is speech related to the prurient or sexual. The Miller Test, derived from the United States Supreme Court case of the same name, has the following criteria:

> (a) whether the "average person, applying contemporary community standards" would find the work, taken as a whole, appeals to the prurient interest; (b) whether the work depicts or describes, in a patently offensive way, sexual conduct specifically defined by the applicable state law; and (c) whether the work, taken as a whole, lacks serious literary, artistic, political, or scientific value. (*Miller v. California* 1972)

Although this is a legal test, it is highly subjective. Deciding if something has value or only appeals to prurient interest is often in the eye of the beholder. As with many legal standards, this determination can only be made by a court after an injured party brings a suit. Although the test refers to community standards and the value of a work, something is only legally obscene if a judge determines it to be so.

Finally, true threats and fighting words are the type of unprotected speech that seem to have the most relevance to the current free speech debate even though these terms are rarely used. True threats and fighting words, as decided in *Chaplinsky v. New Hampshire* (1942), concern words that lead to violence. I provide the following quote from the Supreme Court decision because it demonstrates the decision (which has not been overturned) is very much a product of its time and is not necessarily adequate for addressing the free speech issues of our time.

> The word "offensive" is not to be defined in terms of what a particular addressee thinks. . . . The test is what men of common intelligence would understand would be words likely to cause an average addressee to fight. . . . The English language has a number of words and expressions which, by general consent, are "fighting words" when said without a disarming smile. . . . [S]uch words, as ordinary men know, are likely to cause a fight. So are threatening, profane or obscene revilings [sic]. Derisive and annoying words can be taken as coming within the purview of the statute as heretofore interpreted only when they have this characteristic of plainly tending to excite the addressee to a breach of the peace. . . . The statute, as construed, does no more than prohibit the

face-to-face words plainly likely to cause a breach of the peace by the addressee, words whose speaking constitutes a breach of the peace by the speaker—including "classical fighting words," words in current use less "classical" but equally likely to cause violence, and other disorderly words, including profanity, obscenity and threats [ellipses in original]. (*Chaplinsky v. New Hampshire* 1942)

Along with the use of the gendered language, the Supreme Court at that time also assumed that all members of society would understand what "classical fighting words" are. This is a clear example of the embeddedness of language: few English speakers in the early twenty-first century would understand the historical and philosophical definitions of this phrase.

The *Virginia v. Black* (2003) case defined true threats. This was a case in which the Commonwealth of Virginia had outlawed cross burning, but the Supreme Court found that this law was unconstitutional because it did not take intent into account. Virginia had outlawed all cross burnings and not just those that were intended to intimidate. In addition, the burden of proof must be on the state and not on the defendant. *RAV v. St. Paul* (1992) overturned the city's bias crimes clause for being overly broad. In her work on hate speech, Nadine Strossen (2020, 61) notes that some symbolic actions, such as the presence of a noose on campus, can be considered a true threat.

These exceptions to freedom of expression in the United States are known as unprotected speech and have been established through jurisprudence. In addition, it is important to note that, using the differentiation discussed above, the First Amendment covers and sometimes protects many different kinds of expression. Because it would be impossible to discuss all of the legal cases related to freedom of expression and intellectual freedom here, readers are encouraged to review the list of important cases on the American Library Association's website to learn more about individual cases (see the list of further readings at the end of this chapter).

FREEDOM OF EXPRESSION AND INTERPRETIVE COMMUNITIES

All expression is situated within a given context and is informed by norms and shaped by language. One method for understanding how expression is embedded in language is through what Clifford Geertz (1973) called thick description. He employed the example of knowing the difference between a wink and a twitch even though they are both similar eye movements. In order to know the difference, the interpreter must be immersed within a given community. Although Geertz was focused on ethnographic methods for anthropology, his method provides a foundation for understanding why the interpretation of a particular text or image might vary across national societies and individual communities.

One example of the embeddedness of speech is the use of the terms "BIPOC" or "Black," "Indigenous," and "people of color." About three years ago, I had never heard of this term when it started appearing in articles I was reading for work and I had to look it up. Little did I know that it described me! Of course, BIPOC itself is a term that has come into vogue after other words like "marginalized" or "minority" have received their own critiques since they imply a deficit (Cooper 2016). Another example is the use of "Latinx," a term that is used in more liberal and progressive communities, including academia, but rarely used in the community it describes (Noe-Bustamante, Mora, and Lopez 2020). "Latine" is also a preferred gender-neutral term among some communities (Blas 2019).

When it comes to other types of expression, we can see the existence of interpretive communities when one visits an art museum. For example, Robert Rauschenberg's *White Painting* may be incomprehensible to one visitor to the gallery and profound to another. The Rauschenberg Foundation notes that composer John Cage was inspired to create his famous piece *4'33,* another work of art that requires a particular interpretive strategy to understand as it consists of 4 minutes and 33 seconds of "silence" from the performer (Vartanian 2013).

Outside of the visual, literary, or performing art worlds, protest is another form of expression whose interpretation is often deeply embedded. The destruction of property during protests is an action that is highly controversial and is sometimes interpreted as an expressive act and by others as a crime, depending on the point of view of the interpreter.

Interpretive communities were first introduced by literary theorist Stanley Fish in his book *Is There a Text in This Class?* (1982). He argues that people's experiences give text structure and it is these experiences that create meaning. Individuals use specific strategies to interpret and make meaning of texts. When a group shares a particular strategy for interpreting a text, they form an interpretive community. "These strategies exist prior to the act of reading and therefore determine the shape of what is read rather than, as is usually assumed, the other way around" (Fish 1982, 171). These shared strategies create the practice of reading, the act of writing, the creation of art, and other expressions, and how they are interpreted.

One example of the embeddedness of language and interpretation and how they affect people on an individual level is so-called cancel culture. Like free speech, the phrase "cancel culture" is highly disputed. Some state that it does not exist because it only refers to the consequences that one might receive for engaging in behavior that some find disturbing or immoral. Others state that it does exist because it refers to a form of shunning. Alexandria Ocasio-Cortez (2020), for example, noted on Twitter:

> People who are actually "cancelled" don't get their thoughts published and amplified in major outlets. . . . The term "cancel culture" comes from entitlement—as though the person complaining has the right to a large, captive audience, & one is a victim if people choose to tune them out. Odds are you're not actually cancelled, you're just being challenged, held accountable, or unliked.

In her long-form video essay on the YouTube channel *ContraPoints,* Natalie Wynn (2020) puts forth a fully fleshed out theory of cancel culture that focuses on seven tropes:

1. Presumption of guilt
2. Abstraction
3. Essentialism
4. Pseudo-Moralism
5. Absence of grace (no forgiveness)
6. Transitivity
7. Dualism

Wynn herself has been "canceled"—the video is based on her experience. Notably, she includes all sides of the debate over this issue (Wynn 2020). Professor and activist Loretta Ross (2019) has written extensively on alternatives to cancel culture and argues that people should be "called in":

Calling in is speaking up without tearing down. A call-in can happen publicly or privately, but its key feature is that it's done with love. Instead of shaming someone who's made a mistake, we can patiently ask questions to explore what was going on and why the speaker chose their harmful language.

In the end, cancel culture is an amorphous phrase that has wildly different interpretations depending on who is doing the interpretation. It is, like many things related to freedom of expression, in the eye of the beholder.

FREE SPEECH

Throughout this chapter I have used the term "freedom of expression" rather than "free speech" because, as mentioned above, "free speech" is a contested term in society. In addition, "freedom of expression" allows for wider variates of expressive action, including the fine and performing arts and protest. Free speech, on the other hand, has become weaponized, especially in the online environment. Conservative writers, pundits, and instigators often state that they may say anything they want to because of the right to free speech, even if this speech is harmful to others.

For example, Milo Yiannopoulos, a far-right polemicist, attempted to hold a Free Speech Week at the University of California, Berkeley, which would have included conservative pundits and rallies. It was canceled, according to press releases, due to security concerns. Progressive commentators, on the other hand, argue that speech is always subject to consequences and caution that unfettered free speech harms those without power. Legal scholar Catharine MacKinnon (2019, 141) however, argues that free speech proponents undertheorize power: "Being unable to tell the difference between relative power and powerlessness . . . has become firmly entrenched in the First Amendment, and social discourse invoking it, as the virtue termed 'neutrality,' with the inevitable result of reflecting and reinforcing existing unequal social arrangements."

In a *New York Times* article by Adam Liptak (2018), a conservative lawyer, is quoted:

> "The libertarian position has become dominant on the right on First Amendment issues," said Ilya Shapiro, a lawyer with the Cato Institute. "It simply means that we should be skeptical of government attempts to regulate speech. That used to be an uncontroversial and nonideological point. What's now being called the libertarian position on speech was in the 1960s the liberal position on speech."

(Ironically, Ilya Shapiro himself found himself in hot water with his own comments on Black women nominees to the Supreme Court in 2022.)

"Free speech" is a term that has shifted in meaning over the past few years and is now used as a method of signaling how one feels about speech regulation and consequences. This state of affairs is especially true when it comes to hateful and harmful speech. The question for supporters of intellectual freedom becomes: What should be done in the face of hate speech? What is the proper response to a hate group that wants to use the library's meeting room? Or a hateful book in the collection? In his book *Against Free Speech*, Anthony Leaker (2020, 9) argues that those who argue for free speech do not examine the underlying assumptions about language and power. My hope is that this chapter demonstrates that this is not an accurate assertion. Unfortunately, there are no easy answers; however, the next section of this chapter should provide some explanation for how the free speech/hate speech debate might be considered in the context of intellectual freedom while keeping in mind that librarianship and other information professionals are called on to "affirm the inherent dignity and rights of every person" (ALA 2021).

HATEFUL OR HARMFUL SPEECH AND THE EMBEDDEDNESS OF EXPRESSION

The primary problem with discussing free speech and hate speech is that there is not a shared definition for either of these terms, and an "I know it when I see it" approach is often used to define it. Epithets like the n-word are generally not used in polite society but, as legal scholar Randall Kennedy (2021, 259) notes, who is doing the saying and why they are saying it matters. Using the n-word in rap and hip-hop is very different from when the word is hurled by Proud Boys online or on the street. It is important to keep in mind that the impact of these words is in the eye of the beholder.

All speech, like other types of expression, is situated within interpretive communities, which, in turn give meaning to these expressions. For example, when I give talks or seminars on trigger warnings, I encounter people who are part of decidedly separate interpretative communities even if they live in the same physical community. The people who attend have very different understandings of what trigger warnings are and how they are used. At the same talk I was once asked by one attendee "when should I use a trigger warning versus a content warning?" while another attendee asked (before the talk started) "what is a trigger warning?" These people lived in the same city but obviously had different interpretive communities—one of which used content and trigger warnings on a regular basis whereas the other did not use them at all.

Something similar happens with hate speech. In late 2021 and early 2022 there have been many book challenges across the United States. These challenges are overwhelming to books written by diverse authors or that center on the experiences of underrepresented groups. The challengers in these cases have taken terms like "harm," "racist," and "critical race theory" (CRT) and employed them in their arguments to remove these books. Rather than seeing critical race theory as part of the antiracism movement, conservative parents and commentators argue that CRT itself is racist (e.g., see Overman 2022; "Critical Race Theory Code Words" n.d.). Within these interpretive community, words and movements like "woke" or Black Lives Matter are racist. For example, the Moms for Liberty Chapter of Williamson County (Tennessee) listed every mention of "injustice" in a teacher's manual as a pejorative ("Complaint Filed by Local Moms" 2021). Former president Donald Trump stated that Black Lives Matter was a symbol of hate. This is a phrase he declined to use when referring to the white supremacist rally in Charlottesville, Virginia, in 2017 (Liptak and Holmes 2020).

Another example of the embeddedness of hate speech is the term "TERF" ("transexclusionary radical feminist"). People who are called TERFs argue that the term TERF is a slur and hate speech while trans individuals and allies state the term is not a slur but rather an accurate description of certain ideological and political positions (Flaherty 2018; Murphy 2017; Saul 2020). What constitutes hateful and harmful speech is not agreed upon across all sectors of society.

Some argue that the United States should adopt European-style hate speech laws. Hate speech laws in Europe are complex and differ from country to country as well as in the European Union (EU) as a whole. For example, Germany's hate speech law primarily consists of three statutes. The first states:

> Whosoever, in a manner liable to disturb public peace, (1) incites hatred against parts of the population or invites violence or arbitrary acts against them, or (2) attacks the human dignity of others by insulting, maliciously degrading or defaming parts of the population shall be punished with imprisonment of no less than three months and not exceeding five years. (German Criminal Code, Section 130)

As Winifred Brugger (2002, 5) notes, "the second paragraph of the provision contains a similar prohibition on publications and explicitly defines hate speech by mentioning incitement to hatred against 'groups determined by nationality, race, religion, or ethnic origin.'" Interestingly, Brugger adds, this law was not enough to reduce Holocaust denialism in Germany and a third section was added in 1994. Paragraph three of the section, added in 1994, punishes "whoever, in public or in an assembly, approves, denies or minimizes an act described in §220a(1) [i.e., genocide] committed under National Socialism, in a manner which is liable to disturb the public peace" (Brugger 2002, 5-6). This law was eventually expanded to cover hate speech on the internet. A full overview of various European laws can be found in Sarah H. Cleveland's chapter (2019) in *The Free Speech Century* on how hate speech operates within the international system of human rights.

In the United States, the philosophical argument for imposing hate speech laws began with the series of essays that were eventually collected in the volume *Words That Wound: Critical Race Theory, Assaultive Speech, and the First Amendment* (Matsuda et al. 1993). In one essay, Matsuda argues that "the need to limit racist hate messages is implicit in basic human rights documents such as the UN Charter and the Universal Declaration of Human Rights" (Matsuda 1993, 30). Hate speech should be outlawed because it both gives and leads to physical effects on the body. More recently, others outside of the academy have taken up this argument. For example, in *The Case against Free Speech*, P. E. Moskowitz (2019) argues that current interpretations of the First Amendment uphold white supremacy and inequality.

Unfortunately, although they have the best intentions, hate speech laws often fail because language is slippery. They are also, by definition, reactionary. What constitutes minimization or incitement must be determined by a court. Language and other types of expression, as noted above, are deeply embedded in communities and a seemingly innocuous statement (e.g., "Let's Go Brandon," a code for [expletive] Joe Biden that was popularized in late 2021) can take on a dark undertone. As Fish (2020, 45) notes, one problem with hate speech laws is that they conflate speech and actions. Pro-hate speech law theorists argue:

> If you want to stop hate speech, what you have to do is deny its status as speech and move it over into the category of action, for once this relocation has been effected, the abstract equality of all forms of speech is no longer assumed and a new question can be asked: not *What ideas do these words express?* But *What actions do these words perform?* [emphasis in original].

Fish calls this a structural argument that "tak[es] the speech out of hate speech."

One question that must be answered is whether or not the hate speech laws are effective. For example, the watchdog group ARTICLE 19 found numerous problems with hate speech laws in 2018:

The six country reports identified widespread deficiencies in the respective national frameworks on "hate speech" in terms of their compatibility with applicable international freedom of expression standards, as well as inconsistencies in the application of existing legislation. In ARTICLE 19's view, these deficiencies render the legal framework open to political abuse, including against precisely those minority groups that the law should protect. Moreover, the respective national frameworks generally fail to provide effective remedies to victims of "hate speech," and are insufficient to enable instances of intercommunal tensions to be effectively resolved, or to enable poor social cohesion to be addressed.

The question of who decides what is hate speech and what should be paid back to people who have been harmed is a difficult one. As with many aspects of criminal justice systems, hate speech laws in Europe focus on punishment rather than restoration. They are intended to deter those who would engage in such behavior, but because language is slippery, there are often ways around the law. The case of Aung San Suu Kyi provides an example. Even after suffering and being recognized for human rights violations against herself, she chooses not to recognize the humanity of the Muslim minority Rohingya in her own country testimony before the Hague did not even mention the Rohingya by name (Simons and Beech 2019).

Another example comes from New Zealand where, after the terrorist attack on a mosque in Christchurch in 2019, there was a call to eradicate terrorist and violent extremist online content. A report found that it was difficult to find this material however because "the alt-right commonly cloaks ideology in generalities and uses code and covert signals, irony, sarcasm, images, memes and in-jokes to shroud borderline content and extreme view in plausible deniability" (Bromell 2022, 41-42).

In yet another example, even though Germany has robust hate speech laws, the far-right, anti-immigration party Alternative für Deutschland (AfD) (Alternative for Germany) won 10.3 percent of the nationwide vote in 2021. However, as a *Politico* article notes, this national vote obscures its popularity in the east of the country where the party came in first in the vote in the states of Saxony and Thuringia (Schultheis 2021).

In a study of six member states' hate speech laws, the EU found that:

Hate speech and hate crimes poison societies by threatening individual rights, human dignity and equality, reinforcing tensions between social groups, disturbing public peace and public order, and jeopardising peaceful coexistence. The lack of adequate means of prevention and response violates values enshrined in Article 2 of the TEU. Member States have diverging rules, and national public administrations are torn by *disagreement in values.* [author's emphasis] (Think Tank—European Parliament 2020)

Despite this disagreement, the EU is evaluating adding hate speech and hate crimes to the list of EU crimes (European Commission 2021).

Randall Kennedy addresses the issues of oversight and punishment in one of the essays in *Say It Loud! On Race, Law, History, and Culture* (2021). Following an analysis of a list of ultimatums published by stakeholders at Princeton intended to make the campus more inclusive, Kennedy (2021, 101) questions how the stipulations will be enforced: "How would the antiracism committee demanded by the letter decide whether to investigate a complaint? Having investigated and found an infraction, what kind of discipline would it levy?" He then proposes a series of scenarios that demonstrate how deeply embedded ideas of inclusion and diversity are in a given context. For example, how should one discuss interracial adoption or abortion within the Black community? Who should lead these discussions?

As many note, freedom of expression is about power, but given how ubiquitous racism, sexism, ethnocentrism, ableism, homophobia, and transphobia, along with other bigotries and prejudices, are in society, this power is rarely used in favor of people who are not part of the dominant culture. Along with a lack of shared understanding of language across divisions, it is unlikely that laws against hate speech or harmful knowledge will ever be used to truly support the marginalized. As Jacob Mchangama (2022, 8) notes,

> It is true that the freedom of speech can be used to amplify division, sow distrust and inflict serious harm. But the view that the deep challenges to dignity trust, democracy, and institutions of our splintered age can be overcome by rolling back free speech rests on shaky historical ground.

Why and how both the state and individuals suppress knowledge will be discussed in the next chapter, which focuses on access and censorship.

SUPPORTING FREE EXPRESSION

Support for intellectual freedom does not take place in a vacuum and it is important that people are aware of how words are used both inside and outside of their own interpretive communities. To put it plainly: the problem with outlawing hate speech is that there is no agreement on what hate speech is. In some places, CRT can be construed as hate speech, whereas in others, TERF is hate speech. Some might argue that this is ridiculous, that it is clear that hate speech is only relevant when it is used against those who are marginalized but these people are simply wrong. Stating that someone's interpretation of expression is ridiculous does not change their understanding of what constitutes hate speech. In addition, libraries and other information institutions are embedded in communities where it is possible that members of those communities will judge a book about a trans adolescent to be hate speech or obscene (Schwartz 2022). Or someone may argue that a Black Lives Matter group cannot meet in the library because it is a hate group (Curto 2021).

Those who wish to circumscribe the principle of intellectual freedom must look at the slippery slope consequences for outlawing speech. In the United States, who would have the final say over what is or is not obscenity? As of 2022 the Supreme Court slants 6–3 conservative, and it is unlikely that the current members of the court would support any progressive interpretations of the term "hate speech." As Nadine Strossen (2020, 13) notes, hate speech laws put the power to decide what is hateful into the hands of the government. They also imply that the government will always be on the side of those who have been harmed by hate speech. In his book on freedom of expression, Christopher Finan (2022) reminds readers that dissemination of the abolitionist, feminist, and progressive messages have only been possible because of the country's overall commitment to free speech and assembly. Of course, there were attempts to silence all of these messages but, as Frederick Douglass famously said in 1860:

> To suppress free speech is a double wrong. It violates the rights of the hearer as well as those of the speaker. It is just as criminal to rob a man of his right to speak and hear as it would be to rob him of his money.

Some librarians have called for the profession to discontinue supporting the principle of intellectual freedom. Carrie Wade argues "the idea that 'free speech comes with costs' is a sloppy argument that ignores the ethics of allowing historically marginalized communities to fundamentally exist in public. These are the same lines of discourses that insist on civility and slow measures to affect change" (Wade 2018). I would argue that those who support intellectual freedom and freedom of expression operate within an alternative theory of change—one that does not trust the entrenched racist, heteronormative, gender-conforming, ableist society and governments to operate in the best interests of those who are marginalized. Also, as Jacob Mchangama notes, fear of free speech is often also a fear of people who are less educated or who have lower societal or economic status. "Upon the introduction of new technology that gives access to those previously unheard, the traditional gatekeepers of public opinion fear that the newcomers will manipulate the masses through dangerous ideas and propaganda, threatening the established social and political order" (Mchangama 2022, 6). The current fears of misinformation and disinformation follow a familiar pattern in this respect.

In addition, information professionals should not assume that they know what the effects of certain words will be on a given person. This does not mean that the materials or expression will not cause harm but rather that it is, in fact, impossible to know that a certain expression will definitely cause harm to an individual or group. There are many mitigating factors involved, and information professionals should be mindful of inadvertent harms that may be caused by removing or curtailing expression. Also, engaging in these types of censorship practices is its own expression of power and paternalism. It implies that one person has both the right and the power to decide what will or will not be harmful for another person.

It is important to acknowledge that this current legal and societal state of affairs can be harmful to marginalized communities. As Suzanne Nossel (2021, 128) writes, "the question of when and how speech can inflict actual harm and how heavily to weigh such injury is vexing. If denigrating messages are repeated and pervasive, they can cause psychology damage." It is understandable that a service-oriented profession like librarianship would sometimes argue for the removal of works that might bring harm. However, this act transfers power from the individual patron to the librarian. It also makes the institution more vulnerable to subsequent requests for removal for any reason. Finally, it does not account for the individuality of each person and their own right to self-actualization and dignity. Nossel (2021, 128) goes on to state that "the damaging power of speech hinges on the context, the speaker, and the listener."

This state of affairs can be seen in the book challenges that began to gain steam in late 2021. Almost all of the books that were challenged in the United States during this time and all but one of the books on ALA's Office for Intellectual Freedom Top 10 list of banned books for 2021 are books that can be categorized as diverse. For example, Danika Ellis (2021) wrote an article for the blog *Book Riot* that analyzed the list of 850 books that a Texas legislator argued were harmful and found that 62.4 percent of the 850 books were on LGBTQ+ topics, 14.1 percent were on sex education, and 8.3 percent were on race and racism (the rest were listed as miscellaneous). The targets of these book challenges were not hate speech as understood by members of progressive and liberal circles but hateful or harmful speech as understood by conservatives.

Libraries are gardens and not labyrinths of truth. The following lengthy quotation from Robert V. Labaree and Ross Scimeca (2008, 62) discusses libraries, the historical record, and the problem of truth:

> If one considers all the books that line the shelves of any given library as a collection, including the acquisition of materials for that collection, its accessibility, and its

dissemination, a unique concern about truth is revealed. Consider any given library as a record of humanity's accomplishments and failures. Both the beauty and the ugliness of humanity's history must be represented in this collection. Sadly, however, this balanced perspective about humanity's accomplishments and failures is often compromised by a number of factors. One such factor, often affecting public libraries, is the decision to avoid community outcry concerning controversial material. Such material could be different lifestyle perspectives, negative views of various stages of American or world history, art or literature that is deemed morally offensive, and hate literature. Regardless of the truth value of the propositions and perspectives contained in such controversial literature, the truth value must be suspended so that a complete picture of recorded history is not compromised. If the historical record is compromised, any and all theories of truth would be compromised. To what end would an individual or some group in society want this? Just as it is often said that knowledge is power, the compromising of knowledge puts that power in the hands of the compromiser.

In an article on newly introduced laws that will limit academic freedom in individual US states, Amna Khalid and Jeffrey Aaron Snyder (2022) argue something similar about the purpose of education. It is not about finding a particular truth but asking questions about truths.

Choosing to support freedom of expression is not a neutral act. Librarians and other information professionals are sometimes put in the difficult position of providing information that may be harmful to users. This happens because of power differentials within society. Information professionals can choose to not provide certain types of information, but they are then putting themselves in the position of knowing what is best for their patrons and also opening themselves up to accusations of bias. In addition, it is possible that librarians, in particular, live and work in communities that do not share their values. Their patrons and neighbors might have retrograde and harmful views of race, sexuality, gender, and ability, and it is having strong support for freedom of expression and intellectual freedom that allows for libraries to support people with underrepresented and marginalized identities within such a community.

DISCUSSION QUESTIONS

- How do we understand the relationship between expression and action?
- What are some possible responses to hate speech?
- What is the library's role in protecting freedom of expression and speech? What does this look like in practice?

FURTHER READING

Finan, Christopher M. 2022. *How Free Speech Saved Democracy: The Untold History of How the First Amendment Became an Essential Tool for Securing Liberty and Social Justice*. Lebanon, NH: Truth to Power.

The executive director of the National Coalition Against Censorship provides a concise defense of free speech in this monograph. Of particular interest is his overview of free speech prior to the twentieth century, especially as it was employed by the abolitionist movement.

Kennedy, Randall. 2021. *Say It Loud! On Race, Law, History, and Culture*. New York: Pantheon Books.
> Although all of these essays do not focus on freedom of expression, many do, and Kennedy provides a historical foundation for thinking about free speech in the late twentieth and early twenty-first centuries. Most importantly, he provides update to his monograph on the n-word and its "strange career."

Matsuda, Mari J., Charles B. Lawrence, Richard Delgado, and Kimberlè Williams Crenshaw. 1993. *Words That Wound: Critical Race Theory, Assaultive Speech, and the First Amendment*. Boulder, CO: Westview Press.
> The essays in this book provide a cogent argument for outlawing hate speech. All who are interested in intellectual freedom should examine the authors' arguments.

Mchangama, Jacob. 2022. *Free Speech: A History from Socrates to Social Media*. New York: Basic Books.
> This comprehensive global history of free speech centers on how elites in societies quash expression to entrench their power.

Nossel, Suzanne. 2021. *Dare to Speak: Defending Free Speech For All*. New York: HarperCollins.
> Nossel is the CEO of PEN America, an organization dedicated to free expression in literature. Her overview of the legal typology of harm provides models for understanding what hate speech is.

Strossen, Nadine. 2020. *HATE: Why We Should Resist It with Free Speech, Not Censorship*. New York: Oxford University Press.
> Strossen is a former president of the American Civil Liberties Union, and this book is solely focused on hate speech and some responses to it. She is especially concerned with outcomes of hate speech laws and how they are often ineffective for stemming harmful speech.

REFERENCES

American Library Association. 2021. Code of Ethics. www.ifmanual.org/codeethics.

Article 19. 2018. "Responding to 'Hate Speech': Comparative Overview of Six EU Countries." *Article 19*, March 2018. https://www.article19.org/resources/responding-hate-speech-comparative-overview-six-eu-countries/.

———. 2021. "The Global Expression Report—2021." https://www.article19.org/wp-content/uploads/2021/07/A19-GxR-2021-FINAL.pdf.

Blas, Terry. 2019. "'Latinx' Is Growing in Popularity. I Made a Comic to Help You Understand Why." *Vox*, October 15, 2019. https://www.vox.com/the-highlight/2019/10/15/20914347/latin-latina-latino-latinx-means.

Bromell, David. 2022. *Regulating Free Speech in a Digital Age: Hate, Harm and the Limits of Censorship*. Cham, Switzerland: Springer International Publishing.

Brugger, Winfried. 2002. "Bans on or Protection of Hate Speech? Some Observations Based on German and American Law." *Tulane European and Civil Law Forum* 17. https://journals.tulane.edu/teclf/article/view/1662.

Chaplinsky v. New Hampshire. 1942, 315 US 568. Supreme Court.

Cleveland, Sarah H. 2019. "Hate Speech at Home and Abroad." In *The Free Speech Century*, edited by Lee C. Bollinger and Geoffrey R. Stone, 210–34. Oxford: Oxford University Press. https://public.ebookcentral.proquest.com/choice/publicfullrecord.aspx?p=5567803.

"Complaint Filed by Local Moms for Liberty Chapter Rejected by State." 2021. *Williamson Herald*, November 30, 2021. https://www.williamsonherald.com/features/education/complaint-filed-by-local-moms-for-liberty-chapter-rejected-by-state/article_81146dc4-518f-11ec-9d9a-237001a4ab9f.html.

ContraPoints. 2020. *Canceling*. https://www.youtube.com/watch?v=OjMPJVmXxV8.

Cooper, Joseph. 2016. "A Call for a Language Shift: From Covert Oppression to Overt Empowerment." December 7, 2016. https://education.uconn.edu/2016/12/07/a-call-for-a-language-shift-from-covert-oppression-to-overt-empowerment/.

"Critical Race Theory (CRT) Code Words." n.d. *No Left Turn* (blog). https://www.noleftturn.us/crt-code-words/.

Curto, Justin. 2021. "Former HFPA President Called Black Lives Matter 'Racist Hate Movement' in Email." *Vulture*, April 20, 2021. https://www.vulture.com/2021/04/former-hfpa-president-black-lives-matter-racist-email.html.

Darnton, Robert. 1991. "What Is the History of Books?" In *Kiss of Lamourette: Reflections in Culture*, 107–35. New York: W. W. Norton and Company.

Douglass, Frederick. (1860) 2019. "Frederick Douglass's 'Plea for Freedom of Speech in Boston.'" *Law and Liberty* (blog), August 21, 2019. https://lawliberty.org/frederick-douglass-plea-for-freedom-of-speech-in-boston/.

Ellis, Danika. 2021. "All 850 Books Texas Lawmaker Matt Krause Wants to Ban: An Analysis." *Book Riot* (blog), November 5, 2021. https://bookriot.com/texas-book-ban-list/.

Emerson, Thomas Irwin. 1970. *The System of Freedom of Expression*. New York: Random House.

European Commission. 2021. "The Commission Proposes to Extend the List of 'EU Crimes.'" Text. European Commission—European Commission. December 9, 2021. https://ec.europa.eu/commission/presscorner/detail/en/IP_21_6561.

Farkas, Meredith. 2020. "When Speech Isn't Free." *American Libraries*. May 1, 2020. https://americanlibrariesmagazine.org/2020/05/01/neutrality-when-speech-isnt-free/.

Finan, Christopher M. 2022. *How Free Speech Saved Democracy: The Untold History of How the First Amendment Became an Essential Tool for Securing Liberty and Social Justice*. Lebanon, NH: Truth to Power.

Fish, Stanley. 1982. *Is There a Text in This Class?* Cambridge, MA: Harvard University Press.

———. 2020. *The First: How to Think about Hate Speech, Campus Speech, Religious Speech, Fake News, Post-Truth, and Donald Trump*. New York: Simon and Schuster.

Flaherty, Collen. 2018. "Philosophers Object to a Journal's Publication 'TERF,' in Reference to Some Feminists. Is It Really a Slur?" *Inside Higher Ed*, August 29, 2018. https://www.insidehighered.com/news/2018/08/29/philosophers-object-journals-publication-terf-reference-some-feminists-it-really.

Geertz, Clifford. 1973. *The Interpretation of Cultures: Selected Essays*. New York: Basic Books.

German Criminal Code (Strafgesetzbuch—StGB). n.d. https://www.gesetze-im-internet.de/englisch_stgb/englisch_stgb.html#p1333.

Kennedy, Randall. 2021. *Say It Loud! On Race, Law, History, and Culture*. New York: Pantheon Books.

Khalid, Amna, and Jeffrey Aaron Snyder. 2022. "The Purpose of a University Isn't Truth. It's Inquiry." *The Chronicle of Higher Education*, February 10, 2022. https://www.chronicle.com/article/the-purpose-of-a-university-isnt-truth-its-inquiry.

Labaree, Robert V., and Ross Scimeca. 2008. "The Philosophical Problem of Truth in Librarianship." *Library Quarterly* 78 (1): 43–70. https://doi.org/10.1086/523909.

Leaker, Anthony. 2020. *Against Free Speech*. Lanham, MD: Rowman and Littlefield.

Liptak, Adam. 2018. "How Conservatives Weaponized the First Amendment." *The New York Times*, June 30, 2018. https://www.nytimes.com/2018/06/30/us/politics/first-amendment-conservatives-supreme-court.html.

Liptak, Kevin, and Karen Holmes. 2020. "Trump Calls Black Lives Matter a 'Symbol of Hate' as He Digs in on Race." CNN. July 7, 2020. https://www.cnn.com/2020/07/01/politics/donald-trump-black-lives-matter-confederate-race/index.html.

MacKinnon, Catharine A. 2019. "The First Amendment: An Equality Reading." In *The Free Speech Century*, edited by Lee C. Bollinger and Geoffrey R. Stone, 140–61. Oxford: Oxford University Press. https://public.ebookcentral.proquest.com/choice/publicfullrecord.aspx?p=5567803.

Matsuda, Mari J. 1993. "Public Response to Racist Speech: Considering the Victim's Story." In *Words That Wound: Critical Race Theory, Assaultive Speech, and the First Amendment,* by Charles B. Lawrence, Richard Delgado, Kimberlè Williams Crenshaw, and Mari J. Matsuda, 17–49. Boulder, CO: Westview Press,.

Matsuda, Mari J., Charles B. Lawrence, Richard Delgado, and Kimberlè Williams Crenshaw. 1993. *Words That Wound: Critical Race Theory, Assaultive Speech, and the First Amendment.* Boulder, CO: Westview Press.

Mchangama, Jacob. 2022. *Free Speech: A History from Socrates to Social Media.* New York: Basic Books.

Miller v. California. 1972, 413 US 15. Supreme Court.

Moskowitz, P. E. 2019. *The Case against Free Speech: The First Amendment, Fascism, and the Future of Dissent.* https://www.overdrive.com/search?q=D717DD6C-6164-4D3B-8F94-76C90DFCEBD7.

Murphy, Meghan. 2017. "'TERF' Isn't Just a Slur, It's Hate Speech." *Feminist Current* (blog), September 22, 2017. https://www.feministcurrent.com/2017/09/21/terf-isnt-slur-hate-speech/.

Noe-Bustamante, Luis, Lauren Mora, and Mark Hugo Lopez. 2020. "About One-in-Four U.S. Hispanics Have Heard of Latinx, but Just 3% Use It." *Pew Research Center's Hispanic Trends Project* (blog), August 11, 2020. https://www.pewresearch.org/hispanic/2020/08/11/about-one-in-four-u-s-hispanics-have-heard-of-latinx-but-just-3-use-it/.

Nossel, Suzanne. 2021. *Dare to Speak: Defending Free Speech For All.* New York: HarperCollins.

Ocasio-Cortez, Alexandria. 2020 (@AOC). "People Who Are Actually 'Cancelled' Don't Get Their Thoughts Published and Amplified in Major Outlets. This Has Been a Public Service Announcement." Twitter, July 10, 2020. https://twitter.com/AOC/status/1281388656935284736.

On the Media. 2022. "Political Fictions—January 21, 2022." WNYC. https://www.wnycstudios.org/podcasts/otm/episodes/on-the-media-political-fictions.

Overman, Tom. 2022. "Letter to the Editor: CRT Is Racism." *The Northern Virginia Daily*, February 28, 2022. https://www.nvdaily.com/nvdaily/letter-to-the-editor-crt-is-racism/article_fc1f9781-924c-51c8-9eb8-d7b67cae3c1a.html.

RAV v. St. Paul. 1992, 505 US 377. Supreme Court.

Ross, Loretta. 2019. "Speaking Up Without Tearing Down." *Learning for Justice,* January 2, 2019. https://www.learningforjustice.org/magazine/spring-2019/speaking-up-without-tearing-down.

Saul, Jennifer. 2020. "Why the Words We Use Matter When Describing Anti-Trans Activists." *The Conversation,* March 5, 2020. http://theconversation.com/why-the-words-we-use-matter-when-describing-anti-trans-activists-130990.

Schultheis, Emily. 2021. "Germany's Far-Right AfD Loses Nationally, but Wins in the East." *Politico*, September 28, 2021. https://www.politico.eu/article/german-election-far-right-afd-loses-nationally-but-wins-in-east/.

Schwartz, Jeremy. 2022. "North Texas Superintendent Orders Books Removed from Schools, Targeting Titles about Transgender People." *The Texas Tribune*, March 23, 2022. https://www.texastribune.org/2022/03/23/north-texas-superintendent-targets-books-about-transgender-people/.

Simons, Marlise, and Hannah Beech. 2019. "Aung San Suu Kyi Defends Myanmar against Rohingya Genocide Accusations." *The New York Times*, December 11, 2019. https://www.nytimes.com/2019/12/11/world/asia/aung-san-suu-kyi-rohingya-myanmar-genocide-hague.html.

Strossen, Nadine. 2020. *HATE: Why We Should Resist It with Free Speech, Not Censorship.* New York: Oxford University Press.

Think Tank—European Parliament. 2020. "Hate Speech and Hate Crime in the EU and the Evaluation of Online Content Regulation Approaches." https://www.europarl.europa.eu/thinktank/en/document/IPOL_STU(2020)655135.

Tushnet, Mark V., Alan K. Chen, and Joseph Blocher. 2020. *Free Speech beyond Words: The Surprising Reach of the First Amendment.* New York: NYU Press.

United Nations. 1948. "The Universal Declaration of Human Rights." 1948. www.un.org/en/documents/udhr/.

Vartanian, Hrag. 2013. "The Original: John Cage, '4'33' (In Proportional Notation) (1952/1953)." *Hyperallergic,* September 27, 2013. http://hyperallergic.com/85779/the-original-john-cage-433-in-proportional-notation-19521953/.

Virginia v. Black. 2003, 538 US 343. Supreme Court.

Wade, Carrie. 2018. "Rethinking 'Intellectual Freedom.'" *Library Barbarian* (blog), July 10, 2018. https://seadoubleyew.com/188/rethinking-intellectual-freedom/.

White Painting. 1951. Robert Rauschenberg Foundation. https://www.rauschenbergfoundation.org/art/galleries/series/white-painting-1951.

Wynn, Natalie. 2020. "Transcript of 'Canceling.'" *ContraPoints*. January 2, 2020. https://www.contrapoints.com/transcripts/canceling.

CHAPTER 4

Information Access and Censorship

INFORMATION ACCESS—A CORE PRINCIPLE

In many respects, information access is the most important facet of intellectual freedom. When individuals think about intellectual freedom (as opposed to its converse—censorship), they are often thinking about how they gain access to data, books, journals, treatises, and other types of information. In addition, information access is a core value of librarianship. Information access is the point of bibliographic control and information organization. Why bother cataloging information or creating new metadata schemes if not to make information accessible to those who want or need it?

I have written about information access in a previous work in this series, *Foundations of Information Ethics* (Knox 2019b). For more information on the intellectual history of information access and an overview of current issues, I encourage the reader to review the chapter 3 of that book. The current chapter will focus on the intersection of intellectual freedom and information access to discuss why librarians should provide access to information and some guidelines on how they might go about doing so.

The chapter begins with an introduction to information access and how this concept is both informed and changed by the development of the knowledge society. It then offers a typology of types of access, including the concept of universal design. The chapter also includes an overview of developing policy for intellectual freedom. It ends with a discussion of censorship practices.

WHAT IS INFORMATION ACCESS? WHY DOES IT MATTER?

Article 19 of the United Nations Universal Declaration of Human Rights (1948) focuses on the communication circuit and states that everyone has the right to "seek, receive and impart information and ideas through any media and regardless of frontier." This chapter focuses on the "seek and receive" aspect of this right. The International Federation of Library Associations and Institutions (IFLA) Code of Ethics (2012) combines information access with intellectual freedom. Article 1 states:

ACCESS TO INFORMATION

The core mission of librarians and other information workers is to ensure access to information for all for personal development, education, cultural enrichment, leisure, economic activity and informed participation in and enhancement of democracy.

Librarians and other information workers reject the denial and restriction of access to information and ideas most particularly through censorship whether by states, governments, or religious or civil society institutions.

Prior to the latest update of the Code of Ethics, IFLA also approved a statement on libraries and intellectual freedom. It focuses on libraries as institutions that provide access to information. The first principle states: "Libraries provide access to information, ideas and works of imagination. They serve as gateways to knowledge, thought and culture" (IFLA 1999).

Similar to the IFLA Code of Ethics, Article 1 of the American Library Association Code of Ethics also focuses on information access: "We provide the highest level of service to all library users through appropriate and usefully organized resources; equitable service policies; equitable access; and accurate, unbiased, and courteous responses to all requests" (ALA 2021). Here organization, equitable policies, and equitable access to resources takes center stage. It is no mistake that the first article of both the IFLA and ALA codes of ethics focus on information access and the communications circuit. As noted in chapter 3, Robert Darnton's circuit (1991, 111) moves from author to publisher to printer to shipper to bookseller to reader. It also notes that the author is also a reader themselves.

It is a cliché to say that we live in an information age, but it is difficult to think of a better description of our society. Information communication technologies (ICTs) are ubiquitous and shape the world as we know it. The circulation of knowledge is necessary for the development of the knowledge society. In their article on the knowledge society, Peter Lor and Johannes Britz (2007) explicitly link information access to eschewing censorship of information. They argue that there are four pillars of the information society. The first, ICTs, provide mediums for accessing information and have the ability to increase participation in society. They also note that ICTs are generally affordable although this will be analyzed more in the section below of the digital divide and digital inclusion for all.

The second pillar, content, is based on John Rawls's theory of justice and focuses on who can participate in the knowledge society. In "On Justice as Fairness," originally published in 1985, Rawls proposes two principles for justice: "equality of assignment of rights and liberties" and that inequalities must be compensated (Rawls 2004). These concepts and their relationship to participation in political economy will be discussed more below.

The third pillar that Lor and Britz (2007) discuss, affordability, is often highly influenced by intellectual property rights. The authors argue that these rights must not be used to restrict access to information.

The final pillar, diversity, is discussed in several different ways. One thing they focus on is the diversity of information itself, noting that "diversity of content is affected by censorship" and arguing that "censorship restricts choice and imposes a suspect uniformity" (Lor and Britz 2007, 394).

Any given individual's access to information and knowledge is influenced by many different factors, including the country they live in, their socioeconomic status in that particular country, the area or region in which they live, literacy, educational attainment, and a host of other factors. In her article on libraries and autonomy, Audrey Barbakoff (2010) writes that access to information is vital for human autonomy as it is "instrumentally valuable" for having "the moral capacity to make one's own choices" and notes that autonomy is not all or nothing but involves five competencies: "access to information about many life possibilities, self-reflection, critical thinking, self-worth, and willingness/ability to act" (Barbakoff 2010).

Access to information and other types of expression is an area of intellectual freedom that can be most explicitly linked to social justice. Again, to use Rawls's theory, democratic equality and difference principle states that "unless there is a distribution that makes both persons better off, an equal distribution is to be preferred" (Rawls 2004, 68). It is when one analyzes the differences among an individual's access to information that the injustices of a given society are laid bare. As Rawls (2004, 3) states, "principles of social justice are especially stringent normative standards that apply to what [the individual] terms the basic structure of a society, or those major social, political, and economic institutions that exert a profound and unavoidable impact on its members' life prospects and motivations." In the information age, as we move toward the knowledge society, access to information is vital for human fulfillment and autonomy.

Kay Mathiesen (2008, 574) explicitly links censorship, access to information, and human autonomy: "By promoting access to information, we are enabling the success of such expressive acts by connecting, for instance, the writer and the reader. Second to engage in acts of expression, people need a rich information culture that will allow them to develop their ideas and learn how to communicate them effectively." Mathiesen also offers a nuanced view of why access matters, arguing that it is not speaking that is important but rather that people must be able to communicate, whether via speech or some other medium (Mathiesen 2008, 575). Although these ideas are often conflated, they are not quite the same, and it is important to keep these differences at front of mind when discussing intellectual freedom.

TYPES OF ACCESS

One of the easiest methods for analyzing how people do or do not have access to information is through the digital divide; various groups lack digital inclusion. Although research and activism on the digital divide/digital inclusion focus on information communication technologies (ICTs), the analytical methods used in this sector provide a robust heuristic for understanding other types of information and knowledge divides. Also, note that none of these divides are mutually exclusive.

I will use the terms "digital divide" or "information divide" below, but note that this analysis can hold for any type of knowledge divide. In addition, the term digital divide is contested by scholars as it is a descriptive term that focuses on a technological gulf but does not lead to ameliorative action (Parsons and Hick 2008). As Virginia Eubanks notes, "investment in science and technology without simultaneous investment in a more just society is an investment in increasing political and economic inequality" (Eubanks 2012, xvii). "Digital inclusion," on the other hand, aims to provide people with the tools they need to be part of the knowledge society.

Generally, digital and other information divides operate along several dimensions. First, there are economic divides, which include issues such as the availability of financial resources to support technical and educational infrastructure for providing information. There is also the issue of whether or not individuals have the ability to own their own ICTs. This, not surprisingly, is where libraries come in. Public libraries often provide public access computers so that patrons can find the information they need or want without having to own their own devices. However, libraries themselves are part of the economic divide as their services are dependent on what a community is able to support.

Technical infrastructure and support constitute additional dimensions of the digital divide. This is often discussed as access to broadband, but other aspects of technical infrastructure include servers and storage. Support is key as someone needs to maintain these infrastructures and also help people use them. This is, once again, where libraries are important in supporting information access. It is often the library that not only provides physical access but also has staff trained to help people find the information they need or want.

The skills divide is focused on individuals and whether or not they know how to access information. Institutions like libraries can sometimes have inscrutable rules and norms for finding information. For example, people with the social capital and history of using libraries have tacit knowledge that the fiction section is arranged by last name of author in alphabetical order. This is not necessarily intuitive, however. There is no reason why the fiction section cannot be arranged alphabetically by title. Searching fiction by genre, then author, then by title is a learned skill and must be taught to new generations. Likewise, using the internet means that one must be discerning when it comes to interpreting the information that one finds. Misinformation and disinformation are rife and, once again, developing these skills requires education.

There are also digital divides on the dimensions of gender, race, and income. These are often superimposed with the broader economic divides described above. Geographic divides can be visualized: Where is there broadband? Where are there libraries? This becomes more difficult, however, when one considers that there are not necessarily shared definitions of what constitutes broadband (Ali 2021, 7). It is also important to note that there are both international and intranational divides. The Global North tends to have more access to information and the political structures to support people's use of this information as they see fit. The Global South, often due to historic and current exploitation by the Global North, often does not. However, there are still divides within a given country. Poorer areas in any given nation tend to have less access to digital resources and information more generally.

These divides are important considerations for studying intellectual freedom because they are fundamental for understanding if people are able to access information in the first place. There is a lot of emphasis in the recent discourse on misinformation and disinformation, sometimes to the exclusion of other discussions of information. It is vitally important that librarians and other information professionals continue to focus on making information access a core value because it is vital for human flourishing. The word "ignorance" has a negative connotation, but this is by definition the state that an individual will live in if they live on the wrong side of these divides.

POLICY

Policy has outsized influence in how we live our lives. Why do some people not have healthcare in the United States? Because that was how the policy was written. This is, of course, also a question of politics, but keep in mind that policy is how politics are enacted. This means that policy shapes the structures for how information is provided. It is what ensures that an information institution provides "appropriate and usefully organized resources; equitable service policies; equitable access" to its materials (ALA 2021). Policies act as boundary objects for information institutions and their users or patrons. They "both inhabit several communities of practice and satisfy the informational requirements of each of them" (Bowker and Star 1999, 297). Information policy can be defined as "a broad set of goals—and the accompanying instruments and mechanisms required to accomplish those goals—created by governments and other society institutions to manage the information life cycle (from creation to disposition)" (Jaeger and Taylor 2019, 15). Stakeholders often do not agree on the goals of policy and this can lead to the disparities described above.

More generally, policy can be divided into two types: Big-P and Little-p. In their article "Understanding Evidence-Based Public Health Policy," Ross C. Brownson, Jamie F. Chriqui, and Katherine A. Stamatakis (2009, 1578) state that Big-P policy refers to "formal laws, rules, and regulations enacted by elected officials." Little-p policy, on the other hand, refers to "organizational, internal agency decisions or memoranda, and social norms guiding behavior." Many of the information divides described above can only be solved through Big-P policy through national and international regulation and support. More resources on this type of policy can be found in the recommended reading section at the end of this chapter. In particular, Sandra Braman's (2006) text, which discusses information policy as a method for the state to implement change, is highly recommended. The rest of this chapter is dedicated to Little-p policy for institutions to provide equitable service and access to materials.

Little-p policy is vital for supporting intellectual freedom in local institutions. These policies sometimes intersect with Big-p policy (e.g., the use of the e-rate in US public schools and libraries), but they are often fully developed and implemented locally. One of the best books written on this topic is Sandra S. Nelson and June Garcia's *Creating Policies for Results: From Chaos to Clarity* (2003). Even twenty years after its publication, it is still the best practical guideline for writing policy for any institution even though it is geared toward public libraries. Using their guidelines will help anyone provide equitable services and access to their patrons. Although I have written and discussed Nelson and Garcia's guidelines many times, this chapter will focus on using their recommendations for creating policies to support intellectual freedom in an information institution.

Nelson and Garcia note that good policies have four functions. First, they transform an institution's values into actions. If your institution strives to support intellectual freedom for all, guidelines and practices for facilitating this should be part of your policies. Second, policies provide the information that staff need to perform tasks. How does one ensure that the collection is representative? How does the IT department handle cookies on public access computers? This is all included in policies. Third, policies make sure that "all members of the public know what they can expect from the library and that they are treated equitably" (Nelson and Garcia 2003, 8). This is true for all information institutions. Policies ensure that patrons know what services they will receive when they interact with institutions. Fourth, and finally, policies aid in any legal action against the library. This is one reason why, if at all possible, policies should be reviewed by an attorney and fully vetted by a board or other administrative body.

In addition to these four functions, good policies share three characteristics. They are current, honest, and accessible. Currency is one of the most difficult to achieve as it means that policies must be reviewed on a regular basis to ensure that they are meeting current best practices for access and equity. The IFM, for example, recommends that policies be reviewed regularly (Garnar et al. 2021, 36). Truthfulness in policies can also be difficult. Quite often during the policymaking process, committees attempt to write policies for what they would like to do or what they think they do. As Nelson and Garcia (2003, 6) note, there is often a divide between written policy and "how we do business here." If you do not provide access to certain types of material, this should be included in your policies. Policies should be reviewed to make sure that they reflect what the institution actually does, what the institution's patrons or users think it does, and the language used in the institution's policies. Finally, policies should be accessible. They need to be posted to the institution's website and available in hard copy within the physical building (if there is one). They should be available on demand by anyone who asks for them.

CREATING POLICIES FOR ACCESS AND INTELLECTUAL FREEDOM

One primary issue within librarianship and other information institutions is whether or not policies should be content-neutral. This is solely dependent on the institution and its mission. The mission of a public library, for example, is very different from that of a theological library attached to a seminary. Policies in a private corporation's research department will be different from those in the academic library of a public university. Often the current discourse centers on tax-supported public libraries and schools, but these are not the sole information institutions that need to create policies.

Regardless of the institution, librarians and other information professionals should strive to create policies that lead to the broadest access to information and intellectual freedom for their users and patrons that adhere to the mission of the institution. This is not easy to do as all information institutions have competing obligations and budgetary constraints for providing materials and services. The information below is intended to provide recommendations and strategies for thinking about how an institution's policies will serve all of its users. Staff members are encouraged to review policies from similar institutions and consult manuals such as Nelson and Garcia's *Creating Policies for Results* and the *Intellectual Freedom Manual*. Also, policy development committees must be aware of any international, national, state, and local laws that must be taken into account in policies (e.g., records retention). Librarians and other information professionals are especially encouraged not to create policy in a vacuum. Policies should be fully vetted by other staff members, counsel, and—if applicable—approved by a board. This ensures that many different people review the policy and that it has the symbolic and practical power for enforcement.

According to Nelson and Garcia (2003), policies consist of four parts: guidelines, statements, regulations, and procedures. I will provide a brief overview of each of these in turn with reference to intellectual freedom and information access. The examples are meant to be explanatory and not representative.

Guidelines

Guidelines are not developed by the library or institution itself but are statements from larger organizations or associations, which describe best practices for providing access to materials. Libraries in the United States, for example, are encouraged to use the Library Bill of Rights and its interpretations, and the Freedom to Read and View statements as their policy guidelines. These statements inform users what they can generally expect from the institution. Collection development policies will often reference these statements. Libraries may refer to the IFLA Statement on Libraries and Intellectual Freedom (IFLA 1999). Guidelines provide a framework for developing policies that support access and intellectual freedom for users and patrons.

Policy Statements

Similar to mission statements, policy statements describe *why* a particular service is being offered. For example, my own local public library has the following policy statement at the beginning of its materials selection policy:

> The Champaign Public Library provides a broad range of printed and digital popular materials that support the recreational, educational, and cultural needs of the community. The library's selection of materials sustains the principles embodied in the Library Bill of Rights, and the Freedom to Read and Freedom to View statements, as enunciated by the American Library Association. (https://champaign.org/about/board-policies/materials-selection-policy)

It is important to have a mission statement before embarking on the process of developing policy because the mission statement will help frame all of the elements of the department's written policy. Policy statements help ensure that policies fulfill the third function articulated above by providing information on why a policy exists and how it fits with the overall mission of the institution.

Mission and Vision Statements

Mission statements are important for all institutions but especially those that provide access to information. A mission statement focuses on what you do and allows stakeholders to know the objectives of the institution. A *vision statement* is forward looking and describes what an institution or organization would like to become.

Regulations

Regulations are what most people think of when someone uses the term "policy" in that they describe how a particular policy statement will be carried out. Regulations are most easily understood through examples. To return to my local public library, here is the Library Record Confidentiality regulation:

> It is the policy of the Champaign Public Library, pursuant to the Library Records Confidentiality Act (75 ILSC 70/1), that all circulation, registration, and other records identifying the names of library users and their transactions with the library and while using library resources are confidential. The contents of any such electronic or paper records will not be made available to anyone except the card holder, and to the parent or guardian of a minor child card holder following presentation of photo identification of the parent or guardian. (https://champaign.org/about/board-policies/privacy-and-confidentiality-policy)

Smith College has the following regulations for the library's serial policy:

Some of the factors to consider in adding new subscriptions are:

- Relevance to the curriculum, both existing courses and new directions
- Relevance to faculty scholarship, with preference given to titles needed by more than one person
- Needs of newly hired faculty, to support both new courses and their own scholarship
- Cost of the subscription
- Number and cost of other titles in the field available at Smith
- Accreditation requirements
- Coverage in indexing and abstracting services, Google Scholar, Discover, and other access tools
- Demand as demonstrated by interlibrary loan requests (https://libraries.smith.edu/services/faculty/order-materials/serials-policy)

The Dag Hammarskjöld Library (named for the second secretary general of the United Nations) at the United Nations is only open to the public for research purposes. Its policies are available on its website:

> The services of the Library will also be made available, as far as feasible, to the specialized agencies, accredited representatives of mass media of information, international governmental organizations, affiliated non-governmental organizations, educational institutions, scholars and writers. No one needing to use full sets of the documents and publications of the League of Nations, the United Nations or the specialized agencies will be denied access to the Library. Service to the public, however, must necessarily be subordinated to the service needed by the United Nations. (https://documents-dds-ny.un.org/doc/UNDOC/GEN/NL4/914/76/PDF/NL491476.pdf?OpenElement)

These examples are helpful not only to understand what a regulation is but also to encourage people who are writing policy to search for policy statements and regulations online. Policy is not created in a vacuum and committees should feel free to adapt freely available policies for their own use.

Procedures

Procedures are the most time-consuming part of policy and are often not available publicly. They are a step-by-step overview of how to complete a particular task. Procedures are important because they ensure that multiple staff members will be able to completely describe the steps needed to complete a task even if the person who is regularly assigned to it is not available. Procedures are not needed for all policies but they should be a priority for some library functions. For example, the University of Illinois library posts procedures on the staff section of the website. The procedures for purchasing diversity, equity, inclusion, and accessible (DEIA) materials through EBSCO's GOBI Library Solutions are posted on the staff website under "Acquisitions" (https://www.library.illinois.edu/staff/acquisitions/howto/gobi-deia/).

Writing policy can be difficult and tedious. Although there is usually a committee discussing the policy, as Nelson and Garcia (2003, 89) note: "Committees do not write, individuals write." In addition, policies should be free of jargon and written for the appropriate audience. Policies are important even if a staff member or user refuses to follow them. They provide legal and practical foundations for action, for example, when a staff member needs to be placed on a performance improvement plan or when someone is upset about a book in the school library. It is also important to know that everyone will not follow the written policies, but this does not, however, negate their significance. All institutions that provide information should have written, updated, and accessible policies.

WHICH POLICIES?

The *Intellectual Freedom Manual* (Garnar et al. 2021, 34) recommends the following policies in libraries for supporting intellectual freedom:

- collection development and resource reconsideration
- internet use, use of meeting rooms, and exhibit spaces
- use of meeting rooms and exhibit spaces
- privacy and confidentiality
- social media
- user behavior and library use

Some institutions may choose to create separate policies for resource reconsideration and not combine meeting rooms and exhibit spaces. Focusing on the institution's mission is key here. An art library may need a more comprehensive exhibit space policy than a school library. Non-library institutions may need, for example, more detailed privacy and confidentiality policies. The *Intellectual Freedom Manual* provides a comprehensive checklist for creating all of these policies.

OTHER TYPES OF ACCESS

One of the most important methods for providing access to information is through open government laws that allow citizens to be informed of what their governments are doing. The UN named this as Number 16 of its Sustainable Development Goals: Ensure public access to information and protect fundamental freedoms (UN 2015). There are two indicators for this goal. The first is straightforward: the number of countries that adopt and implement constitutional, statutory, and/or policy guarantees for public access to information. The second indicator reminds us of why intellectual freedom, freedom of the press, and freedom of assembly are so important as it includes the following sobering numbers: the number of verified cases of killing, kidnapping, enforced disappearance, arbitrary detention and torture of journalists, associated media personnel, trade unionists, and human rights advocates in the previous twelve months.

Open Records Laws

In the United States, the Freedom of Information Act fulfills the first indicator of the 16th Sustainable Development Goals. Signed by Lyndon B. Johnson in 1966 after much discussion in Congress, it is based on an original report titled "Clarifying and Protecting the Right of the Public to Information and for Other Purposes." All fifty states and the District of Columbia passed their own versions of the law. These so-called sunshine laws operate in generally the same way: a constituent (as defined by the law) can make a written request to review non-classified government documents. It is important to note that these laws have various levels of efficacy and adhesion. For example, there is no time limit for response to requests for public records in North Carolina while the Illinois Freedom of Information Act requires a response within five days after receiving the request (Oltmann et al. 2016).

Some laws provide an appeals process if the requestor finds fault with the government agency's response. It should be noted that these issues regarding deadlines and appeals have implications for research, as administrative bodies in states without timely response requirements may never respond to a request. In addition, there is the problem of open records harassment wherein the requestor attempts to overwhelm the agency with requests. Public institutions should be aware of the possibility of harassment and put procedures in place for responding.

Depository Libraries

Depository libraries make government documents freely available to stakeholders. Although many documents are now freely available on the internet, the depository system provides direct access to government information for all. In the United States, the federal depository system, which was first established in 1813 and has been part of the Government Publishing Office since 1895, ensures that government documents are locally available (Government Printing Office 2021). States and local municipalities often also follow a depository system.

CENSORSHIP PRACTICES

Another important aspect of understanding intellectual freedom is to consider the various actions that people take to abrogate an individual's right to access information. As Kristin Pekoll notes, "people resist what they don't understand. They challenge the different, the unknown" (Pekoll 2019, xiii). Rather than focusing on whether or not these challenges can all be understood as "censorship," it is helpful to categorize several different actions as censorship practices. I am using "practice" in two senses: first in the sense that it is an "actual application or use of an idea, belief or method," and second in the sense there are shared, regular actions of censorship. Although the ALA definition above includes five practices (suppress, exclude, expurgate, remove, or restrict), I generally divide these into active and passive practices. The active practices are what I call "The 4 Rs": redaction, restriction, relocation, and removal. Passive practices include self-censorship and bias.

Redaction

Redaction refers to obscuring text or images within a work. It is often associated with classified documents but can also be a practice employed outside of government documents to hide text or images that are found to be politically, morally, or socially objectionable.

One of the most notorious cases of redaction took place in 1972 when librarians redacted copies of Maurice Sendak's *In the Night Kitchen* to remove visual depictions of the protagonist's penis (Orlofsky 2019). Redaction is a bit different from defacement, which is a form of vandalism in which someone writes on a text or image but does not necessarily obscure text.

Restriction

Restriction is a common type of censorship practice that needs to be carefully explained. Restricting a work means that it has been removed from access by its intended audience. This last point is very important. In the United States, restriction is often seen through the use of permission slips. For example, children may be able to check out a book on sexual education that is intended for their particular age group but only if they have explicit permission from their parents.

Relocation

Relocation is related to restriction in that it involves impeding access to information by an intended audience. However, in this case, instead of making the barrier to access another person or system (e.g., permission slips), in the practice of relocation, a work is removed from its proper classification and placed into another. For example, books on sexual education that are intended for children are moved to the young adult or "parenting section" of a library. Another example was when *This Book Is Gay* by Juno Dawson was relocated from the teen nonfiction section to the adult nonfiction section in the Lafayette (LA) Public Library in 2021 (KATC 2021).

Removal

Removal is the censorship practice that most laypeople identify as censorship. It is defined as completely removing a work so that it is not accessible. It is difficult to know how many works are actually removed. Most formal challenges or complaints do not result in removal, but it is unknown if works are simply quietly removed from circulation without any discussion.

There have been numerous examples of book removal in the United States in the early 2020s. For example, *Maus* by Art Spiegelman was removed from McMinn County (TN) schools in 2022 (Kasakove 2022). Visual art is also often subject to removal. In 2017, a painting by St. Louis, Missouri, high school student David Pulphus that depicted police violence against Black people was removed by Republican congressional members from the United States Capitol exhibit space without permission (NCAC 2017).

The four practices of redaction, restriction, relocation, and removal are employed by individuals or institutions to inhibit access to information, knowledge, and expression. Engaging in these practices is dependent on using power to create barriers for others. Understanding how power is used to limit or allow access to information is vital to understanding how censorship works as a social phenomenon. This understanding is important to ensuring that individuals' right to intellectual freedom is supported.

Self-Censorship and Bias

People engage in passive censorship practices when they choose not to produce or disseminate knowledge. Self-censorship, for example, happens when a creator decides they are more concerned about the reaction to their creation than creating it. For example, an author may decide not to write a particular novel because it will be censored. Bias is a passive censorship practice wherein someone in power chooses not to purchase or disseminate something because they disagree with it or it makes them uncomfortable. For example, a librarian may choose not to purchase a particular book for their collection because they disagree with its politics even though it is in the scope of their collection development policies.

JUSTIFICATIONS FOR CENSORSHIP

One of the most interesting aspects of censorship practices is trying to understand why and how people justify engaging in the actions described above. This is a subject of much of my research in which I study what I call the discourse of censorship (Knox 2014; 2015; 2017; 2019a). This discourse includes a few themes that I will discuss in brief below; the most interesting aspect of it is that the arguments go against the grain of how we usually think about society. People who are arguing for censorship are arguing against freedom, self-direction, autonomy, and flourishing—things that are highly valued in many societies. As Lester Asheim (1953) writes, for "the censor, on the other hand, the important thing is to find reasons to reject the book; his guiding principle leads him to seek out the objectionable features, the weaknesses, the possibilities for misinterpretation."

In my own research I found three primary themes that people employ when trying to remove materials from public institutions (Knox 2014; 2015). First, they are very concerned about changes in society and worry that the presence of the materials will lead to society's collapse. Next, when arguing for removing materials that are accessible to children, they often draw on ideas of innocence. There are two different conceptualizations of innocence: one focuses on children as blank slates whereas the other focuses on latent bad tendencies already inherent in children's moral character. Materials challenges are also focused on public institutions as symbols of community values. They expect schools and libraries to help parents, especially those who are falling down on the job, to protect children from harm. As I have noted elsewhere (Knox 2014, 177):

> The practice of challenging books has less to do with accessibility per se and is more directly related to issues of community, public institutions, and the practice of reading. For challengers, the presence of a book in a library collection or school curriculum implies that the community—through its institutional proxies—approve of the ideas and concepts presented in the text. It is this implied approval and children's exposure to it that seems to drive challengers' actions toward the futile act of removing, restricting, or relocating a book. It is possible that challengers view the presence of a book in a library collection or school curriculum as an indication that those institutions and, by extension, their communities approve of the concepts found in the text written inside it.

When considering justifications for censoring books, challengers are very attached to the book as a material object that must contain truth. They also argue that there is only one possible interpretation of a text—an interpretation that will lead to a harmful outcome.

INFORMATION ACCESS AND INTELLECTUAL FREEDOM

The importance of information access in the information professions cannot be overstated. As noted, it is the first article in both the IFLA and ALA codes of ethics. The Association for Information Science and Technology's professional guidelines state "ASIS&T members have obligations to employers, clients, and system users, to the profession, and to society, to use judgment and discretion in making choices, providing equitable service, and in defending the rights of open inquiry." The core values and code of ethics of the Society of American Archivists both acknowledge that archivists should "expand access and usage opportunities for users, and potential users, of archival records." Access cannot be separated from intellectual freedom or from social justice. Information professionals must be aware that many of our structures for providing access are embedded in various hegemonic systems of oppression. Miranda H. Belarde-Lewis and Sarah R. Kostelecky (2021, 121-22) note the following when discussing Indigenous relationships to information access:

> The notion of taking control of access to our information and knowledge is not new, but the *enactment of control* in this manner has been a challenge when there are thousands of records, publications, and objects that originated in our community and are now in the care of non-Zuni institutions [emphasis in original].

Only by recognizing when we are engaging in passive censorship practices and not engaging core values and ethics can we ensure that access for all becomes a reality.

DISCUSSION QUESTIONS

- How do we decide what information people should have access to?
- How does this differ for children?
- How should we account for harm when developing collections or curriculum?

FURTHER READING

American Library Association Office for Intellectual Freedom. 1990-present. *Field Report: Banned and Challenged Books*. Chicago: American Library Association.
: The Office for Intellectual Freedom publishes the field report on banned and challenged books every year during Banned Books Week. The bibliography provides short summaries of where and why a book was challenged. The field reports are gathered into a larger comprehensive bibliography every few years.

Bradbury, Ray. 1953. *Fahrenheit 451*. New York: Ballantine Books.
: Bradbury's novel on censorship is a classic. Other books to consider include the middle grade *Ban This Book* by Alan Gratz (Starscape 2017), the YA graphic novel *Banned Book Club* by Kim Hyun Sook (Iron Circus Comics 2020), and the graphic nonfiction *Wake Now in the Fire*, written by Jarrett Dapier (Chronicle Books 2023).

Braman, Sandra. 2006. *Change of State: Information, Policy, and Power*. Cambridge, MA: MIT Press.
: Braman's masterful work on information policy is scholarly but provides a clear overview of how "Big-P" information policy impacts individual lives.

Dick, Kirby, dir. 2006. *This Film Is Not Yet Rated*. Documentary.
   Although this documentary focuses only on movies and not on other types of media, it provides a clear overview on the arbitrariness of labeling. In particular, it explains why the Library Bill of Rights Interpretation on Labeling advocates for mitigating the power of classification to suppress the access to all types of knowledge.

Facts on File Banned Book Series. Various Editions.
   This series of four reference books, *Literature Suppressed on Political Grounds* by Nicholas Karolides, *Literature Suppressed on Sexual Grounds* by Dawn B. Sova, *Literature Suppressed on Religious Grounds* by Margaret Bald, and *Literature Suppressed on Social Grounds* by Dawn B. Sova, provides concise histories of books that have been banned throughout the world.

Gaffney, Lorretta M. 2017. *Young Adult Literature, Libraries, and Conservative Activism*. Lanham, MD: Rowman and Littlefield.
   In recent years, there has been a decided increase in book challenges originating from conservative political groups. Gaffney's monograph provides a clear analysis of how conservative political activism intersects with intellectual freedom for young people.

Jaeger, Paul T., and Natalie Greene Taylor. 2019. *Foundations of Information Policy*. Chicago: ALA Neal-Schuman.
   Another volume in the same series as this book, Jaeger and Greene Taylor provide a wide-ranging overview of information policy. They focus on both Big-P and Little-p policy and include thoughtful discussion of how policies relate to human rights and social justice.

Morrison, Toni, ed. 2012. *Burn This Book: Notes on Literature and Engagement*. New York: HarperCollins.
   Edited by the great Toni Morrison, this volume of essays and meditations discusses the power of the written word from the perspective of authors.

Nelson, Sandra S., June Garcia, and Public Library Association. 2003. *Creating Policies for Results: From Chaos to Clarity*. Chicago: American Library Association.
   This book is a straightforward manual for writing policy—a process that is often opaque. Although it was published twenty years ago, its recommendations are still relevant for writing policy in any institution.

REFERENCES

Ali, Christopher. 2021. *Farm Fresh Broadband: The Politics of Rural Connectivity*. Cambridge, MA: MIT Press.

American Library Association. 2021. Code of Ethics. www.ifmanual.org/codeethics.

Asheim, Lester. 1953. "Not Censorship but Selection." *Wilson Library Bulletin* 28 (1): 63-67.

Barbakoff, Audrey. 2010. "Libraries Build Autonomy: A Philosophical Perspective on the Social Role of Libraries and Librarians." *Library Philosophy and Practice* (January 2010). https://digitalcommons.unl.edu/libphilprac/463/.

Belarde-Lewis, Miranda H., and Sarah R. Kostelecky. 2021. "Tribal Critical Race Theory in Zuni Pueblo: Information Access in a Cautious Community." In *Knowledge Justice: Disrupting Library and Information Studies through Critical Race Theory*, edited by Sofia Y. Leung and Jorge R. López-McKnight, 111-28. Cambridge, MA: MIT Press.

Bowker, Geoffrey, and Susan Leigh Star. 1999. *Sorting Things Out: Classification and Its Consequences*. Cambridge, MA: MIT Press.

Braman, Sandra. 2006. *Change of State: Information, Policy, and Power*. Cambridge, MA: MIT Press.

Brownson, Ross C., Jamie F. Chriqui, and Katherine A. Stamatakis. 2009. "Understanding Evidence-Based Public Health Policy." *American Journal of Public Health* 99 (9): 1576-83. https://doi.org/10.2105/AJPH.2008.156224.

Darnton, Robert. 1991. "What Is the History of Books?" In *Kiss of Lamourette: Reflections in Culture,* 107–35. New York: W. W. Norton and Company.

Eubanks, Virginia. 2012. *Digital Dead End: Fighting for Social Justice in the Information Age.* Cambridge, MA; London: MIT Press.

Garnar, Martin, Trina Magi, and Office for Intellectual Freedom, eds. 2021. *Intellectual Freedom Manual.* 10th ed. Chicago: American Library Association.

Government Printing Office. 2021. "A Brief History of the FDLP." December 15, 2021. https://www.fdlp.gov/about/mission/a-brief-history-of-the-fdlp.

International Federation of Library Associations and Institutions. 1999. "IFLA Statement on Libraries and Intellectual Freedom." https://repository.ifla.org/bitstream/123456789/1424/1/ifla-statement-on-libraries-and-intellectual-freedom-en.pdf.

———. 2012. "IFLA Code of Ethics for Librarians and Other Information Workers (Full Version)." www.ifla.org/publications/node/11092.

Jaeger, Paul T., and Natalie Greene Taylor. 2019. *Foundations of Information Policy.* Chicago: ALA Neal-Schuman.

Kasakove, Sophie. 2022. "The Fight Over 'Maus' Is Part of a Bigger Cultural Battle in Tennessee." *The New York Times,* March 4, 2022. https://www.nytimes.com/2022/03/04/us/maus-banned-books-tennessee.html.

KATC. 2021. "Book about Growing Up Queer Will Stay on Lafayette Library's Shelf." Radio broadcast, November 16, 2021. https://www.katc.com/news/lafayette-parish/book-about-growing-up-queer-will-stay-on-lafayette-librarys-shelf.

Knox, Emily J. M. 2014. "Society, Institutions, and Common Sense: Themes in the Discourse of Book Challengers in 21st Century United States." *Library and Information Science Research* 36 (3): 171–78. www.sciencedirect.com/science/article/pii/S074081881400053X.

———. 2015. *Book Banning in 21st-Century America.* Beta Phi Mu Scholars. Lanham, MD: Rowman and Littlefield.

———. 2017. "Indoctrination and Common Sense Interpretation of Texts: The Tucson Unified School District Book Banning." *Journal of Intellectual Freedom and Privacy* 2 (2): 11–22. https://doi.org/10.5860/jifp.v2i2.6246.

———. 2019a. "Silencing Stories: Challenges to Diverse Books." *The International Journal of Information, Diversity, and Inclusion (IJIDI)* 3 (2).

———. 2019b. "Information Access." In *Foundations of Information Ethics,* edited by John T. F. Burgess and Emily J. M. Knox, 37–46. Chicago: ALA Neal Schuman.

Lor, Peter Johan, and Johannes Jacobus Britz. 2007. "Is a Knowledge Society Possible without Freedom of Access to Information?" *Journal of Information Science* 33 (4): 387–97. https://doi.org/10.1177/0165551506075327.

Mathiesen, Kay. 2008. "Censorship and Access to Expression." In *The Handbook of Information and Computer Ethics,* edited by Kenneth Einar Himma and Herman T. Tavani, 573.

NCAC. 2017. "NCAC Condemns Decision to Remove Student Painting from U.S. Capitol Building; Update: Rep. Clay Files Lawsuit against Architect of the Capitol." *National Coalition Against Censorship* (blog), January 19, 2017. https://ncac.org/news/blog/ncac-condemns-decision-to-remove-student-painting-from-u-s-capitol-building.

Nelson, Sandra S., June Garcia, and Public Library Association. 2003. *Creating Policies for Results: From Chaos to Clarity.* Chicago: American Library Association.

Oltmann, Shannon M., Emily J. M. Knox, Chris Peterson, and Shawn Musgrave. 2016. "Using Open Records Laws for Research Purposes." *Library and Information Science Research* 37 (4).

Orlofsky, Vicky Ludas. 2019. "Maurice Sendak and the Librarians: When Censorship Came from Within." *Intellectual Freedom Blog* (blog), June 10, 2019. https://www.oif.ala.org/oif/maurice-sendak-and-the-librarians-when-censorship-came-from-within/.

Parsons, Cheryl, and Steven F. Hick. 2008. "Moving from the Digital Divide to Digital Inclusion." *Currents: Scholarship in the Human Services* 7 (2). https://journalhosting.ucalgary.ca/index.php/currents/article/view/15892.

Pekoll, Kristin. 2019. *Beyond Banned Books: Defending Intellectual Freedom throughout Your Library*. Chicago: American Library Association.

Rawls, John. 2004. "On Justice as Fairness." In *Social Justice*, edited by Matthew Clayton and Andrew Williams, 49-84. Malden, MA: Blackwell Publishing Ltd.

United Nations. 1948. "The Universal Declaration of Human Rights." www.un.org/en/documents/udhr/.

———. 2015. Sustainable Development Goals. https://sdgs.un.org/goals.

CHAPTER 5

Privacy and Intellectual Freedom

UNDERSTANDING PRIVACY

Privacy is one of the primary facilitators of intellectual freedom as it allows for individuals to learn new knowledge without fear of reprisal. Although privacy is considered of utmost importance for knowledge or information that has serious bearing on people's lives, it is also important for knowledge associated with leisure. For example, consider the increase in sales of romance novels after the adoption of the e-book reader (Flood 2011). When e-readers were introduced, no one knew what you were reading because the cover of the books were no longer visible to others. You could read Beverly Jenkins or Bertrice Small to your heart's delight without worrying about the judgment of people who noticed your book cover. Although the original data is no longer available, a *Book Riot* summary notes that the website authorearnings.com specifically found that privacy was instrumental to the increased sale of romance books:

> Unfortunately, many romance readers have experienced unwanted attention, questions, or criticism when they buy or read romance in public. While paper romance covers usually telegraph genre, no one knows what you're reading on an ereader. And you can buy and own erotic romance without worrying about who sees you doing it, or your young kids getting hold of it. Sure, many romance readers don't give a rat's ass about this, but for those that do, digital books are most welcome. (Tripler 2016)

Some might scoff at the idea that intellectual freedom has anything to do with romance novels; however, an important aspect of supporting intellectual freedom is understanding that it is not only about information related to education or democracy. All knowledge, including knowledge for play or leisure, is covered by intellectual freedom principles and users deserve privacy in every realm.

Like information access, privacy is also included in the American Library Association Code of Ethics (2021) in Article 3, which states: "We protect each library user's right to privacy and confidentiality with respect to information sought or received and resources consulted, borrowed, acquired or transmitted." Note that this article separates privacy and confidentiality. These concepts (along with anonymity) are related but not the same. Privacy, which is the focus of this chapter, is a people-centered idea that concerns how much control a person has over information. Privacy is essentially about power. Confidentiality is a data-centered concept that focuses on disclosure, which, basically means that an entity will not disclose data. That data is held *in confidence*. Anonymity is also a data-centered concept that focuses on how data is identified. Anonymous data does not have any identifiers attached to it.

Most current research on privacy focuses on individual data but, in keeping with the argument throughout much of this book, support for intellectual freedom demands a broader view of how and why a particular individual's search for information remains private. Chilling effects on intellectual freedom must be avoided, and self-censorship is often the outcome of surveillance cultures. Rather than search for new ideas, people turn within themselves and often on each other.

This chapter focuses on privacy and power and how these relate to intellectual freedom. It then examines the intersection of privacy, security, surveillance, and convenience. It considers the intersection of privacy and power through two theories—one from legal scholar Daniel Solove and another from information scientist Helen Nissenbaum. Finally, the chapter discusses several privacy issues in information institutions.

> **Personally Identifiable Information and Identifiers**
>
> *Personally identifiable information* (PII) is data that can be traced to a particular person. There are two types of identifiers: direct and indirect. *Direct* identifiers include information that is unique to a given person, including age, birth city, and address. *Indirect* identifiers are an amalgam of data points, such as an uncommon job in a given area, that combined together can point to an individual.

THE PRIVACY, SECURITY, SURVEILLANCE, AND CONVENIENCE CYCLE

Privacy, security, surveillance, and convenience are interdependent. We often give up privacy for convenience and tolerate surveillance for convenience. All of these concepts are important for thinking about intellectual freedom and possible repercussions that might come about from powerful people, institutions, or governments knowing what information people are accessing.

As noted, privacy is a people-centered concept that focuses on how much control an individual has over their information. Security has more technical meanings, but as it relates to intellectual freedom, security refers to whether or not someone is able to gain access to information that you prefer that they not have access to. "Surveillance" is an evocative word that brings to mind Orwell's *1984* and Big Brother watching everything you do. The word itself comes from the French for "over watch."

Torin Monahan (2011) notes that surveillance studies are based in Foucault's *Discipline and Punish*, especially his work on the panopticon. Monahan also argues that there has been a move from the study of those who were doing the surveilling to those who were surveilled. He states that surveillance can be defined as "the systematic monitoring of people or groups in order to regulate or govern their behavior" (Monahan 2011, 498). This is a neutral argument that posits that surveillance is neither good nor bad.

Christian Fuchs (2021, 142), on the other hand, has this to say about surveillance and Facebook:

> Facebook is a capitalist company that operates as a surveillance machine. It accumulates capital with the help of targeted personalized advertising. . . . Social networking sites are especially suited for targeted advertising because they store and communicate a vast amount of personal data, and the likes and dislikes of users, which allows them to identify and calculate what products the users are likely to buy.

Fuchs and other scholars like Shoshana Zuboff (2020) use critical theory to understand surveillance in the digital age and how it affects individuals.

When analyzing the intersection of privacy and intellectual freedom, it is clear that many people will trade their privacy for security and convenience, and this often happens through surveillance. Sometimes this trade is coerced, but it is often a choice that is made due to ambivalence. For example, many people use Amazon to purchase books or use the company's smart device, Alexa, because it is easy to do (Bass 2019). Amazon monitors prior purchases and will recommend items, including books, that match a customer's taste. This is clearly a form of surveillance, but people are often willing to give up their privacy for the convenience of having a book delivered quickly to their doorstep.

PRIVACY AND POWER

In his article memorably titled "I've Got Nothing to Hide," Daniel Solove (2007) notes that privacy and power are intricately linked. The problem with the statement "I've got nothing to hide" that some people make when they hear that they are being surveilled by the government or corporations is that it focuses on concealment of personal information. However, hiding is only one aspect of privacy. Solove (2007, 756) argues that privacy is not simply about concealment but is a "set of family resemblances—a plurality of things." More specifically, privacy is about power relations between and among people and the modern state.

This is well-described in Christena Nippert-Eng's book *Islands of Privacy* (2010), where she uses ethnographic methods to understand how people construct themselves on the beach of the islands of privacy. Nippert-Eng also argues that privacy is not simply one thing but has several different meanings. Her subjects touched on three common themes: (1) the ability or power to control access and dissemination; (2) a condition of the body, that is, being alone or without invasions; and (3) "the freedom to do/live make decisions, without regulation/restriction" (Nippert-Eng 2010, 7). Nippert-Eng also notes that privacy must be "managed" because it is not the same in all contexts.

In a special issue on privacy in the *Black Scholar* published in 2021, several authors touched on what privacy means within the Black community, especially when it comes to having an interior intellectual life. For example, in an article on Black women and policing, Christen A. Smith (2021, 20) notes:

> Black women have never known the luxury of privacy in the Americas. Impossible privacy is one of the tormenting dimensions of slavery and its afterlives. White supremacy meets us at every turn. Our every move is stalked and surveilled. Our bodies, our homes, our children, even our graves are not our own; able to be raided, poked, prodded

or stolen at any moment. . . . White supremacy stalks us. Haunting our interior and exterior lives, leaving us no moment of respite or peace—no breath of fresh air.

Although we often think of privacy as something that happens only to information about someone, it is also embodied. That is, privacy affects not just the intellect or information that is held outside of our brains but also the body itself.

In many respects, Solove (2011) focuses on concepts of privacy rather than a single notion of privacy. He offers a full taxonomy of privacy that I will discuss in some depth here as I believe it is useful for understanding the intersection of intellectual freedom and privacy. There are four categories within the taxonomy that he describes in his original article and subsequent book (Solove 2011). The first, information collection, focuses on how data is gathered. It includes both surveillance and interrogation. I would also argue that information collection includes issues of consent. Does the person know that their information is being collected in the first place?

The second category is information processing, which includes storage and the analysis or manipulation of data. It entails information aggregation, identification, insecurity, secondary use, and exclusion. Information identification is of particular concern when it comes to intellectual freedom.

Information dissemination constitutes the third category in Solove's taxonomy. This includes breaches of confidentiality, disclosure and exposure of information, increased accessibility, appropriation, and (my favorite) blackmail. Blackmail clearly demonstrates how privacy is related to power. When someone blackmails another individual, they are exerting their power and control over another person's privacy. Interestingly, blackmail is important for intellectual freedom because of the risk that there might be reprisal for someone else's knowledge that you have read or written something that they find objectionable and attempt to hold this over you. Although it seems hyperbolic, threats of blackmail and disclosure are also related to self-censorship. What will happen if someone finds out that you were looking at a book about a marginalized identity that you may or may not have?

The fourth category is information invasion, which includes intrusion, such as when someone invades a private home, and decisional interference. The latter relates to how those in power can intervene in decisions that individuals make about themselves.

In her book *Privacy in Context*, Helen Nissenbaum (2009) provides another theory for thinking about privacy, especially in the online environment. Nissenbaum argues that context and how information flows are key for understanding how people both protect their privacy online and how they would like other stakeholders to protect their individual information. What people are looking for, Nissenbaum (2009, 2) argues, is appropriate flow of information: "What people care most about is not simply *restricting* the flow of information but ensuring that it flows *appropriately*, and an account of appropriate flow is given [in her book] through the framework of contextual integrity."

According to Nissenbaum, most research on privacy focuses on privacy as a right. She uses a sociotechnical studies lens to explore how privacy is about relationships and power and how it is inherently social (Nissenbaum 2009, 10). Although her theory is focused on online privacy, it provides robust theory for thinking about privacy offline, especially in the age of the pandemic and the resulting need for laws and guidelines concerning vaccine information. Nissenbaum provides three categories of problems with information technology and privacy: monitoring and tracking, aggregation and analysis, and dissemination and publication. The theory of contextual integrity focuses on "context-relative information norms," each component of which is described in part III of her book. Briefly, Nissenbaum's theory focuses on the idea that social context matters for understanding which rules should be used in a given situation and how they should be applied. Contextual integrity is "preserved when information norms are respected when information norms are breach" (Nissenbaum 2009, 140).

A real-world example related to the pandemic is helpful to understand Nissenbaum's theory and the heuristic described below. As an employee of the University of Illinois, I was part of a huge medical experiment called SHIELD, centered on the saliva-based covid-SHIELD test. All students, faculty, and staff were part of the SHIELD program, which was developed to reduce and track SARS-CoV-2 transmissions. (More information is available on the program's website at https://shieldillinois.com.) Along with rapid saliva tests, the SHIELD team also developed a mobile phone application called SaferIllinois for monitoring. Some privacy norms were preserved in the app. For example, you were able to toggle on or off location information that would be used by the SHIELD team if you received a positive test for COVID-19. However, it was necessary to disclose some health information to use the app effectively. For instance, all vaccination information could be added to the application so that you were not required to test.

One of the most useful aspects of Nissenbaum's (2009) work is her decision heuristic. There are two forms: the first provides a baseline while the second is a bit more complicated. These heuristics are important for intellectual freedom as they provide a method for thinking about whether or not a given policy or practice provides adequate protection for individual privacy.

The first heuristic has five steps. When thinking about privacy, first establish the prevailing context. What kind of privacy do people expect in a given situation? In a library, for example, patrons generally expect that their records will be confidential. Second, establish who the key actors are in a given context. Although some actors are obvious (patrons, administrators), some are less so. In a public library, for example, the county council might be a key actor as it might control the library's budget. Special libraries may have to answer to shareholders and not simply to the immediate users. The heuristic's third step is to determine what attributes are affected. This means looking at the specifics: What information will be shared? Who will have access to the information? Fourth, it is necessary to establish change in principles of transmission. This is one that I

Nissenbaum's Augmented Contextual Integrity Decision Heuristic

1. Describe the new practice.
2. Identify the context.
3. Identify the agents.
4. Identify the transmission principles.
5. Locate the norms and any points of departure.
6. Do a *prima facie* assessment.
7. Evaluation I—moral and political factors
8. Evaluation II—systems and practices
9. Make a decision based on contextual integrity. (Nissenbaum 2009, 182)

felt acutely when I signed up for the SaferIllinois mobile app during the COVID-19 pandemic. All of a sudden, my health status was shared not only with my doctor but also with the people running the app within the university. In many respects I had to decide to trust that they would do what was necessary to protect my health information. Finally, the heuristic calls for red flagging any problems, that is, this new practice should be noted and evaluated if it "violat[es] entrenched informational norms and constitutes a prima facie violation of contextual integrity" (Nissenbaum 2009, 149-50).

Nissenbaum notes that contextual integrity is a conservative theory because it does not seek to establish new norms. It looks, instead, at prior norms and similar contexts for providing privacy protection. In fact, she argues, any new practices must be found to be morally superior to the practices that came before (Nissenbaum 2009, 165). In the second heuristic, Nissenbaum augments the first by adding a few more steps to consider. What is most important about Nissenbaum's theory is that it provides a straightforward model for thinking about privacy in many different situations, including those where an individual's right to intellectual freedom may be affected. When thinking about privacy and intellectual freedom, Solove's theory provides an understanding of why it matters, while Nissenbaum provides a method for thinking through what to do.

OTHER PRIVACY CONTEXTS

It is difficult to address all of the different situations in which one's privacy may be restricted. Readers are encouraged to review the recommended reading section at the end of this chapter. In addition, this chapter is informed by privacy in the US context. The interaction of privacy, surveillance, and security works very differently in other countries. One example is China, where the government maintains control over the country's internet and maintains a social credit system. Libraries and other information institutions around the world are continually concerned with issues of privacy, especially when data is so easily disseminated across computer-based systems. This section will provide an overview of some privacy contexts that are relevant to intellectual freedom.

The Right to Be Forgotten

One of the more interesting types of privacy laws that has emerged over the past decade is the so-called right to be forgotten. At first glance, this right is straightforward—as the person whom entities extract data from, I have the right to take that data back if I choose. Jeffrey Rosen (2012) writes that there are three categories that exist under this legal concept. First, if I post something online, do I have the right to delete it? Second, if I post something online and someone reposts it, can I delete it? Third, if someone else posts something about me, do I have the right to delete it or, in other words, make a takedown request? When discussed this way, the implications for intellectual freedom and freedom of expression in particular are clear. However, according to Rosen, there are two different conceptualizations of this right. In the United States, there is an emphasis on free speech; whereas in the European Union, the effects on free speech are downplayed. Bennett (2012) argues that it would be difficult for this right to exist in the United States. For example, there is the problem of newsworthy events and whether or not the subject can take down a news article that might, for example, paint them in an unflattering light.

The General Data Protection Regulation (GDPR) (discussed in more detail below) has a more limited right to erasure under which "an individual can require a data processing entity like Google to de-index, or remove, personal information from its online search results so that the information is no longer accessible via its search engine" (Garnar et al. 2021, 215). The GDPR does hold that this request "shall not apply to the extent that processing is necessary

(a) for exercising the right of freedom of expression and information" (https://gdpr-info.eu/art-17-gdpr/). It is unclear, however, what the effect of the law will be over time.

Safiya Noble (2018) notes that the current conceptualization of the right to be forgotten laws is inadequate as it has been primarily a neoliberal, individualized argument. Noble calls for these laws to "extend beyond the take down of personal information and beyond erasing the memory of past acts from the web. The right to be forgotten must include the recognition of all forms of records that Google is archiving and sharing with third parties, both visible and invisible to the public" (Noble 2018, 131). At the moment, the right to be forgotten requires that each individual request that their information be taken down, but it is important that there continue to be pressure on these companies to develop policies that take the privacy needs of all of their users into account.

Information professionals are encouraged to keep abreast of the latest developments regarding the right to be forgotten laws. For example, there is some research related to public support for these laws. In the United States, the Pew Research Organization found that most Americans support the right to be forgotten; however, such a regulation does not exist in the United States and a European Union Court found in 2019 that Google does not have to apply the law outside of the EU (Auxier 2020).

Protecting Personal Data

Over the past decade or so, several new laws have been passed that greatly affect how individuals relate to their online data. As noted above, the GDPR includes regulations on the right to be forgotten. It is important to understand the overall regulation's relationship to privacy. The GDPR applies only to the European Union, but this might surprise anyone who visits websites on a regular basis. Like any regulation it has problems, but I firmly believe that, due to its ubiquity on the internet, it is one of easiest avenues for considering how one's data is obtained and used by corporate entities. The ubiquity of cookies means that someone or something can see what you are doing on the web. This leads to philosophical questions, such as whether or not intellectual freedom, especially when it comes to gaining new knowledge, is possible online. The section on privacy in information institutions below will discuss some mitigation practices that can be implemented to increase privacy for yourself and your patrons online.

The GDPR replaces the Data Protection Directive 95/36/EC and has three purposes: First, it is intended to harmonize data privacy laws across Europe. Second, it is meant to protect and empower all the data privacy of EU citizens. Finally, it was designed to "reshape the way organizations across the region approach data privacy." The GDPR accomplished this last goal in unexpected ways. Article 4 of the GDPR defines personal data as follows:

> "Personal data" means any information relating to an identified or identifiable natural person ("data subject"); an identifiable natural person is one who can be identified, directly or indirectly, in particular by reference to an identifier such as a name, an identification number, location data, an online identifier or to one or more factors specific to the physical, physiological, genetic, mental, economic, cultural or social identity of that natural person.

It also defines "processing" as being both automated and non-automated. A file cabinet serves as a method for processing according to the GDPR.

It is a testament to our interconnected world that no matter where you are on the globe, you will run into regulations that apply only in the EU when you visit a website. This is because websites do not reside in countries, per se. The passage of the GDPR meant that any company with business in the EU must follow the GDPR. In recent years, we have all become accustomed to having to decide what to do when we receive an "Accept Cookies" notice.

To better explain the impact of the GDPR on tracking data, consider the example of Squarespace, a website design and hosting company based in New York City. Even though they are based in the United States, Squarespace provides services for clients around the globe, some of whom—in turn—also provide services for clients around the globe. This means Squarespace has two audiences for GDPR regulations: people who use their services and the people who use the services of those people. When the GDPR came into effect, Squarespace set up a page explaining the GDPR to their clients and discussing their actions to ensure compliance with the regulation (https://support.squarespace.com/hc/en-us/articles/360000851908-GDPR-and-Squarespace). Along with updating their terms of service and privacy policy and giving customers more control over their data, they note that even though all customers can unsubscribe from their marketing emails at any time, only EU and UK customers can opt out at signup. In addition, Squarespace published a list of best practices for their customers to consider on their own websites. These include conducting a data audit and creating or updating a privacy policy. Squarespace also created a "Cookie Banner" that customers can add to their sites (https://support.squarespace.com/hc/en-us/articles/206545727).

Cookie banners are now ubiquitous across the internet thanks to the GDPR. Most of the time, many of us simply click "Accept All Cookies," but readers should consider clicking on "more information" first to see what information is being collected and how it is being processed. This is a favorite exercise in my social informatics course as it moves people out of their comfort zone and forces them to think a bit more about their own data. For example, the website for University of Illinois (Illinois.edu) is comprehensive and straightforward. The website has four categories of cookies (strictly necessary, performance, functional, and targeting) that are defined in dropdown menus and can be changed. Clicking on "more information" leads to the university's cookie policy. The scope states:

> This Cookie Policy applies to the University of Illinois System and supplements the University of Illinois System Privacy Statement, as well as the University of Illinois Supplemental Privacy Notice, which addresses the privacy rights of persons in the European Economic Area and the United Kingdom pursuant to the European Union General Data Protection Regulation ("GDPR"). The information provided in this Cookie Policy is consistent with the GDPR. (https://www.vpaa.uillinois.edu/resources/cookies)

Even a university in the middle of the corn and soybean fields of Illinois had to comply with an EU regulation.

As with the right to be forgotten, the ongoing implications of the GDPR remain to be seen. In any case, the GDPR offers a visible entry point for encouraging the public at large to think more carefully about the data that is collected and used while they are going about their everyday lives. Information professionals would do well to incorporate the affordances it brings into their professional practices.

The United States does not have a comprehensive data protection law. However, individual states have been working to address the issue of data protection and privacy. Note

The General Data Protection Regulation—GDPR

The GDPR can be read in its entirety online. It is also a bedtime story on the Calm App (https://blog.calm.com/blog/once-upon-a-gdpr). Calm notes that the GDPR is:

- Over 43 times longer than the American Declaration of Independence.
- 214 times longer than the Gettysburg Address by Abraham Lincoln.
- Nearly 420 times longer than the UK Parliament's Bill for triggering Article 50, leading to withdrawal from the EU.

that these are often focused on individuals as consumers. California passed the California Consumer Privacy Act (CCPA) in 2018 and because many businesses have headquarters or do business in California, it has affected the collection of consumer data on a wide scale even though it applies only to residents of California. One of the most significant differences between the GDPR and the CCPA when it comes to data protection is that the CCPA allows for opt-out provisions while the GDPR requires opt-in. California also passed the California Privacy Rights Act (CPRA) in 2020, which strengthened many provisions of the CCPA and brought it more in line with the GDPR.

One non-consumer data privacy protecting law is the Health Insurance Portability and Accountability Act (HIPPA), which protects health records. However, given the United States' for-profit healthcare system, one could argue that HIPPA is also a consumer data protection law. The Children's Online Privacy Protection Act (COPPA) is why social media and online service companies generally do not allow anyone under thirteen to sign up for their services. COPPA requires that children aged twelve and under have explicit consent from a parent or guardian to sue online services. There are also several financial data protection laws in the United States, including those that are part of the Fair Credit Reporting Act and the Sarbanes-Oxley Act. Information professionals should be familiar with these and other laws that relate to their professional practice often in consultation with legal counsel.

Privacy for Minors

What does it mean to have privacy when you are not an adult and do not have autonomy over your body? Minors are, by definition, under care of their legal parent or guardian. I am using the word "minor" here because it has a different valence from children, youth, or teenagers. If we accept that intellectual freedom leads to autonomy, it is important that people under the age of majority have the privacy to explore new knowledge that is important to them.

The positionality of minors with regard to their privacy has long been an ethical issue for librarians and other information professionals. Wyatt (2006, 77) argues that librarians have an ethical duty to protect children and that minimal monitoring of, in this case, internet usage is warranted:

> Most parents feel that the library is a safe place for their children. If librarians do not want the responsibility of monitoring children in the library, then they need to

prominently post notices to the parents that they do not monitor the children at all. Then, parents, who have been warned, can ensure that their children do not visit the public library without a parent or supervising adult. Parents who want their children to have unfiltered access to the Internet can obtain Internet access for them under the parent's log-in or allow them unfiltered Internet access at home. Either way, the parent will not have the false impression that someone is monitoring their children when they are not.

Parental rights are always tightly entwined with minors' rights. Richard Price (2021, 81) notes that there is not a clear understanding of parental rights in the United States:

> [The Supreme Court of the United States] has not developed the doctrine around parental rights clearly. Lower courts have consistently rejected parental rights claims in curricular decisions. For example, when parents asserted a constitutional right to exempt their children from any lesson that even mentioned homosexuality, the First Circuit held that parents do not have a constitutional right to dictate the content of a public school's curriculum.

It is unclear, given the current political climate in the United States, if this interpretation of the law will stand if brought before the courts.

Internet filtering was discussed in chapter 4, but it is important to note that filtering of any sort always involves some violation of privacy. By definition a filter monitors which sites a patron searches for in a browser even if the filter does not allow the site to be displayed for viewing. ALA's Interpretation of the Library Bill of Rights on Minors and Online Activity notes that protecting minors' privacy rights online is of utmost importance but also notes that "prohibiting minors from using social media or participating in online communities prevents youth from engaging in opportunities to learn and develop skills needed for responsible speech online, civil engagement, and personal-privacy protection" (Garnar et al. 2021, 133).

Also of importance is protecting minors' rights to privacy when it comes to reading. For some children, receiving their first library card is one of their first public autonomous acts. The card is theirs and has their name on it. The books and other materials that they would like to engage with are checked out to them. It is important to protect the privacy of these records for many reasons. A classic case would be making sure that a child can check out a book on abuse without worrying that their abuser knows about it. As noted in the *Intellectual Freedom Manual* "many states . . . chose to protect the confidentiality of all library users' records without regard to the library user's age, or the funding, ownership, or control of the library" (Caldwell-Stone 2021).

Privacy in Information Institutions

In many respects it is up to libraries and other information institutions and entities to take an active stance in protecting their users' privacy. This is not because users do not care about privacy but because how one goes about protecting privacy can be unclear. Different systems, both in "real life" and online, require different strategies, and it can be difficult for the average user to know the best methods. Some easy examples include things like developing a robust privacy policy and making sure it is accessible to all stakeholders.

The Data Scientist Association has a code of professional conduct that focuses on obligations to clients and the confidentiality of data. It might serve as a guideline for developing privacy policies in some contexts. A couple of the most interesting aspects of the code are these two exceptions to confidentiality:

> A data scientist may reveal information relating to the representation of a client to the extent the data scientist reasonably believes necessary:
>
> (1) to prevent reasonably certain death or substantial bodily harm;
> (2) to prevent the client from committing a crime or fraud that is reasonably certain to result in substantial injury to the financial interests or property of another and in furtherance of which the client has used or is using the data scientist's services. (https://www.datascienceassn.org/code-of-conduct.html)

Note that the focus on bodily as opposed to other types of harm is reminiscent of arguments for hate speech laws.

For librarians, there are several interpretations of the Library Bill of Rights and resolutions related to privacy from the American Library Association. The *Intellectual Freedom Manual* notes how vital privacy is to the right to intellectual freedom: "the freedom to read and receive information is unlikely to survive if one's reading, research, and online activity are monitored and made known to the government or to the public" (Caldwell-Stone 2021, 206). Libraries and other information must be aware of national and state laws when creating policies. ALA also has specific privacy guidelines for school libraries. Along with reviewing their own policies, these institutions must also be cognizant of the privacy policies of vendors that are used for services.

In *User Privacy: A Practical Guide for Librarians,* Matthew Connolly (2018, 2) argues that there are five major threats to privacy: "malicious hackers, government and legal agencies, advertisers and marketers, networked devices, and user behavior." Responding to each of these can be difficult. Consider taking a privacy audit. How are library records processed? How are on-hold materials displayed? Have all staff members been trained on protecting users' privacy? Organizations such as the Library Freedom Project provide tools and methods for making sure that users' privacy is not violated. Also, consider more low-tech options such as installing privacy filters on public access computer monitors.

Library Freedom Project—libraryfreedom.org

The Library Freedom Project started in 2015 with a project installing a Tor relay in a public library in New Hampshire. The project's mission statement is:

> Privacy is essential for democracy. We provide librarians and their communities with the skills necessary to turn ideals into action. Our community of LFP privacy advocates work collaboratively to drive policy, teach stakeholders, and enact change. Our work is informed by a social justice, feminist, anti-racist approach. We believe in the combined power of long-term collective organizing and short-term, immediate harm reduction to mitigate the harms of living in a surveillance society.

Librarians are also encouraged to review the information on the Library Freedom Project's website regarding surveillance and privacy in libraries. The Library Freedom Project offers free courses on both internal library policy and teaching users and community members about privacy. The website also has several free resources (all posted on GitHub) for improving privacy policies, including an easy-to-use vendor privacy policy checklist.

CONCLUSION

Privacy, like so many issues in intellectual freedom, is complex. It is not just one thing related to concealment but a constellation of practices. In addition, privacy is about power. In such a complex world, balancing privacy, security, and convenience is difficult. It is up to information professionals to make sure that individual's privacy is protected to the greatest extent possible in order to make sure that people are able to exercise their right to intellectual freedom without fear that their privacy will be compromised.

DISCUSSION QUESTIONS

- Use Solove's typology and one of Nissenbaum's decision heuristics to purchase a readers' advisory database and/or analytics for a public library.
- Do you feel comfortable going to the LGBT section of the bookstore? How about the African American section? The romance section? The religion section? Why or why not? How does this relate to privacy?
- Do you agree that privacy is weakened for intellectual activities because there is no difference between public and confidential records?
- How should privacy, security, surveillance, and convenience be balanced?
- Wyatt argues that librarians have an ethical duty to protect children even if it compromises their privacy. Do you agree?

FURTHER READING

Gajda, Amy. 2018. "Privacy, Press, and the Right to Be Forgotten in the United States." *Washington Law Review* 93 (1): 201-64. https://heinonline.org/HOL/P?h=hein.journals/washlr93&i=207.
This article provides a legal overview of the right to be forgotten and its possible ramifications on press freedom.

Greenwald, Glenn, and Ewen MacAskill. 2013. "NSA Prism Program Taps in to User Data of Apple, Google and Others." *The Guardian*, June 7, 2013. www.theguardian.com/world/2013/jun/06/us-tech-giants-nsa-data.
This is the original article that disclosed the information from Edward Snowden regarding the NSA PRISM program. The Wikipedia page on the disclosures is also highly recommended (https://en.wikipedia.org/wiki/Global_surveillance_disclosures_(2013%E2%80%93present).

Jones, Meg Leta. 2016. *Ctrl + Z: The Right to Be Forgotten*. New York: NYU Press.
Jones provides a scholarly analysis of the right to be forgotten in this monograph.

Keen, Caroline. 2022. "Apathy, Convenience or Irrelevance? Identifying Conceptual Barriers to Safeguarding Children's Data Privacy." *New Media and Society* 24 (1): 50-69. https://doi.org/10.1177/1461444820960068.

> This article provides qualitative data from interviews analyzing how children think about their privacy online.

Nissenbaum, Helen. 2009. *Privacy in Context: Technology, Policy, and the Integrity of Social Life.* https://doi.org/10.1515/9780804772891.

> Nissenbaum's monograph provides a straightforward method for thinking about privacy in online environments.

Solove, Daniel J. 2011. *Nothing to Hide: The False Tradeoff Between Privacy and Security*. New Haven, CT: Yale University Press.

> Solove's book focuses on the power relationships that come into play when protecting individual privacy.

The Black Scholar, volume 51, number 1 (2021).

> There is very little in the information field written about underrepresented people and privacy outside of analysis of AI surveillance. Most of what is available focuses on health information. This special issue of the *Black Scholar* focuses on, as the issue's editors, Samantha Pinto and Shoniqua Roach, state, "transformative possibilities of Black privacy in relationship to this moment of hypervisibility."

REFERENCES

American Library Association. 2021. Code of Ethics. www.ifmanual.org/codeethics.

Auxier, Brooke. 2020. "Most Americans Support Right to Have Some Personal Info Removed from Online Searches." *Pew Research Center* (blog), January 27, 2020. https://www.pewresearch.org/fact-tank/2020/01/27/most-americans-support-right-to-have-some-personal-info-removed-from-online-searches/.

Bass, Lauren. 2019. "The Concealed Cost of Convenience: Protecting Personal Data Privacy in the Age of Alexa Notes." *Fordham Intellectual Property, Media and Entertainment Law Journal* 30 (1): 261-324. https://heinonline.org/HOL/P?h=hein.journals/frdipm30&i=267.

Bennett, Steven C. 2012. "The 'Right to Be Forgotten': Reconciling EU and US Perspectives." *Berkeley Journal of International Law*. https://doi.org/10.15779/Z38V08Z.

Caldwell-Stone, Deborah. 2021. "Privacy and Confidentiality: A Deeper Look." In *Intellectual Freedom Manual*, edited by Martin Garnar et al., 10th, 206-24. Chicago: American Library Association.

California Consumer Privacy Act (CCPA). 2018. State of California—Department of Justice—Office of the Attorney General. October 15, 2018. https://oag.ca.gov/privacy/ccpa.

Connolly, Matthew. 2018. *User Privacy: A Practical Guide for Librarians*. Lanham, MD: Rowman and Littlefield.

Flood, Alison. 2011. "Romantic Fiction's Passion for Ebooks." *The Guardian*, October 10, 2011. https://www.theguardian.com/books/2011/oct/10/romantic-fiction-ebooks.

Fuchs, Christian. 2021. *Social Media: A Critical Introduction*. Thousand Oaks, CA: Sage Publications.

Garnar, Martin, Trina Magi, and Office for Intellectual Freedom, eds. 2021. *Intellectual Freedom Manual*. 10th ed. Chicago: American Library Association

"General Data Protection Regulation (GDPR)—Official Legal Text." 2018. General Data Protection Regulation (GDPR). May 25, 2018. https://gdpr-info.eu/.

Monahan, Torin. 2011. "Surveillance as Cultural Practice." *The Sociological Quarterly* 52 (4): 495-508.

Nippert-Eng, Christena. 2010. *Islands of Privacy*. Chicago: University of Chicago Press.

Nissenbaum, Helen. 2009. *Privacy in Context: Technology, Policy, and the Integrity of Social Life*. Stanford, CA: Stanford University Press. https://doi.org/10.1515/9780804772891.

Noble, Safiya Umoja. 2018. *Algorithms of Oppression: How Search Engines Reinforce Racism*. New York: New York University Press.

Price, Richard S. 2021. "Navigating a Doctrinal Grey Area: Free Speech, the Right to Read, and Schools." *First Amendment Studies* 55 (2): 79-101. https://doi.org/10.1080/21689725.2021.1979419.

Rosen, Jeffrey. 2012. "The Right to Be Forgotten." *Stanford Law Review*, February 13, 2012. https://www.stanfordlawreview.org/online/privacy-paradox-the-right-to-be-forgotten/.

Smith, Christen A. 2021. "Impossible Privacy." *The Black Scholar* 51 (1): 20-29. https://doi.org/10.1080/00064246.2020.1855090.

Solove, Daniel J. 2007. "'I've Got Nothing to Hide' and Other Misunderstandings of Privacy." SSRN Scholarly Paper ID 998565. Rochester, NY: Social Science Research Network. http://papers.ssrn.com/abstract=998565.

———. 2011. *Nothing to Hide: The False Tradeoff Between Privacy and Security*. New Haven, CT: Yale University Press.

Tripler, Jessica. 2016. "Why Romance Readers Love Digital Books." *Book Riot* (blog), August 11, 2016. https://bookriot.com/why-romance-readers-love-digital-books/.

Wyatt, Anna May. 2006. "Do Librarians Have an Ethical Duty to Monitor Patrons' Internet Usage in the Public Library?" *Journal of Information Ethics* (Spring 2006): 70-79.

Zuboff, Shoshana. 2020. *The Age of Surveillance Capitalism: The Fight for a Human Future at the New Frontier of Power*. New York: PublicAffairs.

CHAPTER 6

Copyright and Intellectual Freedom

ANY DISCUSSION OF INTELLECTUAL PROPERTY (IP), and copyright more specifically, is always fraught. Intellectual property is a rabbit hole in the legal system where even a cursory exploration immediately opens up a vast array of additional topics. In addition, copyright law in the United States will soon be part of a political and legislative fight. Before January 1, 2024, when Mickey Mouse, for which Disney holds both the copyright and the trademark, becomes part of the public domain there will be a flurry of legislative activity. Although it is not discussed much in the popular media, the outcomes of the 2022 midterm congressional elections and the leadup to the 2024 presidential election will have profound implications for copyright law in the United States. In addition, there will be new developments regarding all aspects of IP discussed at the many upcoming meetings of the World Intellectual Property Organization as its 193 member states continue to grapple with the digital environment (WIPO n.d.).

At first glance, it can be difficult to see how copyright intersects with intellectual freedom. However, it becomes clear once one considers, for example, that digital rights management software governs how users are able to access information on information communication technologies (ICTs). In fact, along with the legal frameworks for freedom of expression and privacy, it is helpful to think of intellectual property law as the third leg of a three-legged legal stool that supports structures for intellectual freedom. IP, and more specifically copyright law, governs who may access what information and in what manner they may do so.

**World Intellectual Property Organization (WIPO)—
www.wipo.int/portal/en**

Along with privacy, intellectual property is one of the aspects of intellectual freedom that is most intertwined with international law. WIPO, established in 1967, has 193 member states. It is an umbrella organization that holds regular meetings of its decision-making bodies. The United States has been a member since 1970 and is a party to many treaties administered by WIPO (https://wipolex.wipo.int/en/treaties/ShowResults?search_what=B&country_id=179C).

Article 19 of the United Nations Universal Declaration of Human Rights (1948) states that the right to freedom of expression includes the right to "receive and impart information and ideas through any media and regardless of frontiers." How one receives and imparts information and ideas is bound up in the structures of national and international copyright law and, with the rise of the internet, "regardless of frontiers" has truly become a reality. In addition, the American Library Association Code of Ethics bluntly states in Article IV that "We recognize and respect intellectual property rights" (ALA 2021). The Association for Information Science and Technology (ASIS&T) professional guidelines more delicately affirm that it is the information professionals' responsibility to "respect whatever proprietary rights belong to [users], providers, or employers" (Association for Information Science and Technology 1992).

This chapter begins with a short overview of intellectual property and its four constituent parts: trademarks, patents, trade secrets, and copyright. It then provides a short overview of copyright law in both the US and international context including *droit moral*. This section includes a short history of copyright with an emphasis on Anglo-American law. Primarily for efficiency, the chapter focuses on copyright law in the United States and will only briefly discuss non-US legal frameworks. It provides a short overview of both exceptions to copyright including right of first sale and fair use along with copyright alternatives, including the open access movement and Creative Commons. The focus of the chapter is on the relation of these topics and how they provide structure for people to access information and ideas but not necessarily procedures for policy development. Readers are strongly encouraged to review the additional resources listed at the end of the chapter.

INTELLECTUAL PROPERTY, *DROIT MORAL*, AND COPYRIGHT

To understand how copyright law provides a framework for information access, it is necessary to provide an overview of the history of intellectual property law. It may seem abstract, but ideas of intellectual property are fully embedded in the concept of property itself. Property is not a universal concept, and there are societies that do not have any mechanisms for recognizing property that belongs to an individual. This is important because current intellectual property law is often taken as a given, but there are alternative structures for understanding who owns a particular work and how it should circulate. These range from what might be considered radical from a Western point of view (all works should be owned by everyone in given society) to the more limited (shortened copyright terms). In any case, intellectual property schemes structure the circulation of ideas and information.

The terms "intellectual property" and "copyright" have been used interchangeably in this chapter so far, but they are not the same. Intellectual property is the broader term that categorizes a type of property that is the product of human creativity. Copyright is a narrower term for a type of intellectual property that, along with trademarks and patents, accounts for much of the IP law in the Global North. Trade secrets are sometimes added as a fourth type. Each of these types of IP has its own legal history and structure, and each one is its own rabbit hole into legal arcana. Briefly, patents are the legal rights to ideas (as opposed to copyright—ideas cannot be copyrighted) and generally apply to machines, processes, products, and matter compositions. Trademarks are words or symbols that designate a particular source of goods or services. They include both word marks and design marks. Trade secrets are defined by the World Intellectual Property Organization (WIPO) as "intellectual property rights on confidential information which may be sold or licensed" ("Trade

Secrets" n.d.). There are three requirements for IP to count as a trade secret according to the WIPO definition. First, the IP's secretiveness makes it commercially valuable. Second, very few people know about the secret. Third, the secret holders work to keep the IP secret using tools such as nondisclosure agreements. Copyright, at its most basic, refers to who has the right to copy a work.

Droit moral or moral rights are related to but different from copyrights. *Droit moral* refers to the rights of a creator to their work (Crews 2020, 31). For the purposes of understanding intellectual freedom, *droit moral* allows, for example, for works to be published anonymously or pseudonymously to protect the creator's identity. In the United States, explicit moral rights only apply to visual art, but moral rights are implied in other parts of the Copyright Code. In other countries, moral rights are the foundation of copyright law. Another concept is the *droit de suite,* which allows for royalties for resale.

Intellectual property is governed by legal structures, but it is also a philosophical concept. What does it mean to be the creator of a work? Who owns a work when it is published? Are buildings creative works? How do you copyright performance art? Who has the right to circulate a given image? How much should someone pay the creator for their work? What if you can't find the creator of a work? It all very quickly moves into philosophical territory. Although many laws are reactionary, IP law is extraordinarily so because creativity and dissemination of works circulate and change much more quickly than legislative and statutory structures.

Copyright is highly relevant to intellectual freedom and will be the focus of this chapter. As stated above, it refers to its constituent parts—who has the right to copy a work. Although the history of copyright law has been debated, its development can be traced to printers in Renaissance Italy who had the right to copy works. Eventually copyright law spread across Europe to England, where in 1662, printers were given a monopoly over publishing through the Licensing Act. This meant that non-licensed individuals could be prosecuted for printing pamphlets and books. The act lapsed three years later, but Parliament eventually passed the Statute of Queen Anne in 1710. Rather than give printers copyright, the statute transferred copyright to authors and also established a fixed term of fourteen years for copyright protection (Gilmer 1994). (As a quick aside, the copyright term in the United States is now life of the author plus an additional seventy years.) There are some who argue that fourteen years is the optimal term.[*]

Copyright is often about balance—balancing the rights of creators with the rights of users. It is always difficult to create this steady state, and issues of copyright are often political with many deep-pocketed stakeholders on one side and many who are unaware of how much copyright law shapes their lives on the other.

COPYRIGHT IN THE UNITED STATES

The Statute of Anne was the law in the English colonies in North America until the Revolutionary War. French and Spanish colonies followed *droit d'auteur/derechos de autor*/rights of the author. If anyone ever doubts the importance of copyright, it should be noted that

---

[*] It is also not known why multiples of seven are ubiquitous in copyright law, although I suspect this has to do with the Jubilee Year cycle as laid out in the Book of Leviticus.

the framers of the United States Constitution believed that copyright was so important that they included it in Article 1, Section 8: "The Congress shall have Power . . . To promote the Progress of Science and useful Arts, by securing for limited Times to Authors and Inventors the exclusive Right to their respective Writings and Discoveries."

Even though copyright was important to the governmental framers and representatives of the new nation, they did not pass any national laws specifying how to carry out the Article's remit on exclusive rights. Instead, each state had its own laws governing copyright until 1790, when Congress passed the first Copyright Act, which was based on the Statute of Anne.

In the years since, the act has only been fully revised four times—in 1831, 1870, 1909, and 1976—although it has been amended many times. The years more or less correspond with major changes in US society and changes in communication technology. Lobbyists have always played a major part in the revision of the law. Noah Webster, of dictionary fame, successfully lobbied for the copyright term to be extended from fourteen to twenty-eight years in the 1831 law (Davis 2019). Following the Civil War, the 1870 law transferred the copyright office to the Library of Congress. There had been radical changes in communication technology since 1870, and the 1909 law grappled with the ideas of fixity and authorship. It also extended the copyright term to fifty-six years.

In Europe the Berne Convention of 1886 "established mutually satisfactory uniform copyright law to replace the need for separate registration in every country" ("Copyright Timeline: A History of Copyright in the United States" n.d.). The United States did not sign onto the Berne Convention until 1988. Samuel Jacobs (2016) argues that this is due to the differing philosophical foundations of copyright law in Europe and the United States. *Droit moral* has its basis in natural law whereas copyright law in the United States is based in utilitarianism. In 1893, the United International Bureaux for the Protection of Intellectual Property (BIRPI) was formed by the combination of two organizations that grew out of the Berne Convention and the Paris Convention for the Protection of Industrial Property. BIRPI became the World Intellectual Property Organization in 1967 and was absorbed by the United Nations in 1967, not long before the final full revision of the United States Copyright Act in 1976.

THE 1976 COPYRIGHT ACT AND INTELLECTUAL FREEDOM

The 1976 Copyright Act revision was highly influenced by the development of the mimeograph and the copy machine. What does it mean to hold copyright when there is a device that can easily copy any printed material? As we shall see, this conundrum was only exacerbated by the rise of the personal computer. The 1976 law increased the copyright term to life of the creator plus fifty years (fear not, the ubiquitous sevens will return!). It also included provisions that moved the United States closer to the statutes of the Berne Convention by allowing for all works that are "fixed" to have copyright protection even if they do not include a copyright notice. Fixed refers to works that are in a "tangible form of expression" ("Copyright" n.d.).

The act provides copyright protection to "original works of authorship fixed in any tangible medium of expression, now known or later developed, from which they can be perceived, reproduced, or otherwise communicated, either directly or with the aid of a machine or device." Note that it still uses the term "author" rather than "creator." Although this book will be mostly concerned with literary works, the act also covers literary, music, dramatic, choreographic, art, movies, sound recordings, and eventually architectural works. As I noted above, it is easy to see how questions of copyright can quickly move into "what is art?" territory.

Because the 1976 Copyright Act is still the law of the land as of the publication of this book, this act and its relationship to intellectual freedom are discussed in some detail below. The copyright law of the United States is Title 17 of the United States Code. Readers are encouraged to at least skim through Title 17 to see how expansive it is. Chapters 1-8 and 10-12 of Title 17 focus on copyright proper. Chapter 9 focuses on semiconductor chips.

There are several statutes in the 1976 Copyright Act that are relevant to intellectual freedom. These are related to ownership and transfer of copyright, copyright notices, infringement, and the overall duration of copyright. These are important because they structure how intellectual freedom is supported (or not supported) in US society. In many respects, copyright is an invisible gate for receiving and giving information. First, Chapter 2 of Title 17 uses the term "author" throughout, but for the purposes of understanding copyright and intellectual freedom in the digital age, it is important to think of an author as the creator. Section 201 notes that copyright is vested in the author or authors of a work. If we think back to Article 19 of the UN Universal Declaration of Human Rights, we can see that copyright law and its conceptions of ownership have clear implications on receiving and imparting information through any media. There are more rabbit holes in Chapter 2 of the law, including "Works Made for Hire" and "Collective Works." The former refers to the work created when you work for someone else. For example, does an instructor own their syllabus or does the university that they work for? Chapter 2 also discusses transfer of ownership of copyright. I, the author of this book, have the copyright for it. When I write research articles for scholarly journals, copyright is usually transferred to the journal. However, I remain the creator of the work and retain moral rights to my articles.

The Copyright Act of 1976 states that works are copyrighted when they are fixed. There is no need to apply a copyright notice. As Kenneth Crews (2020, 49) notes:

> One of the most sweeping concepts of modern copyright law is the easiest and clearest to apply. The breadth and scope of the provision, however, also extend the reach of the law far beyond where copyright protection may be warranted or even desired. Consider the profundity of this principle: Copyright protection vests immediately and automatically upon the creation of "original works of authorship" that are "fixed in any tangible medium of expression." Under that provision, copyright protection applies instantly to nearly every e-mail, vacation photo, scribbled missive, and rant on Twitter. These works can easily meet the test of originality, and they are fixed in a tangible medium when penned to paper or saved to a computer drive or photographed with a smart phone. The result is an abundance of copyrighted works, without any further requirement of a copyright notice, registration, or any other step.

It is difficult to overstate the importance of this provision. Many more works are protected by copyright than most laypeople realize. This has profound implications for access and circulation of information. Your personal journal is protected by copyright as are your children's thousands of selfies.

Most commercially published material contains a copyright notice of some sort. For example, while writing this book, an online used book shop sent me the middle-grade book *The Case of the Missing Carrot Cake* written by Robin Newman and illustrated by Deborah

Zemke (2015) instead of sending *How Institutions Think* by Mary Douglas. The Newman book has a standard copyright notice:

> All rights reserved. NO part of this book may be reproduced in any form or by any electronic or mechanical means including information storage and retrieval system—except in case of brief quotations embodied in critical articles or reviews—without permission in writing from its publisher, Creston Books, LLC.

The "information storage and retrieval system" refers to search tools to Google Books or Amazon's "Look Inside" feature project. A quick search reveals that only a snippet preview of the book is available in Google Books: https://www.google.com/books/edition/A_Wilcox_and_Griswold_Mystery_the_Case_o/6Q-EDwAAQBAJ?hl=en&gbpv=0. The snippet preview is common for books that are still under copyright. Along with a standard copyright clause, the book also includes a cute but important legal disclaimer on its copyright page:

> Although thoroughly tested for safety and deliciousness, no recipe is foolproof: bake carefully and with adult supervision. Creston Books, LLC, is not responsible for any loss, injury, cake theft, frosting mess, or somnambulance resulting from following the recipe in this book.

Note that even though the author and the illustrator retain their respective copyrights to the book, it is the publisher, Creston Books that would be liable for any mishaps related to following the recipe in the book.

Along with changes in the copyright notice, the 1976 Copyright Act also extended the duration of copyright. This is a bit complicated, but for works that had not entered the public domain prior to 1978, copyright was extended to life of the author plus fifty years. Non-public domain works published before 1978 were increased to a total of seventy-six years. This long copyright duration is important for understanding the intersection of intellectual freedom and copyright. An effective term of approximately 120 to 130 years means that works remain in copyright for a very long time and cannot be remixed or reused without permission of the creator even if the creator is no longer alive. This will be discussed more below.

Copyright infringement is a criminal act. This is the overall structure of the copyright that informs how freedom of expression is understood in any given society. Users can be sued for copyright infringement and heavy fines can be assessed. The 1976 law included fair

---

The United States Copyright Office

The Copyright Office is one of the service divisions of the Library of Congress and is run by the Register of Copyrights. This is important as there have been struggles to move the office out of the Library of Congress into a different federal department. For people who care about intellectual freedom, having the Copyright Office in a library can make a difference when it comes to access to information. When Dr. Carla Hayden became Librarian of Congress, there was a push to move the office out of the Library Congress to the executive branch (Albanese n.d.).

use provisions. Although it is not necessary to register a work with the United States Copyright Office in order for it to be protected by copyright law, the work must be registered to sue for copyright infringement. The threat of lawsuit is one of the major issues that intertwines intellectual freedom and copyright. Creators are often hesitant to use works if they are unsure of the copyright status.

COPYRIGHTS, FAIR USE, AND INFRINGEMENT

As mentioned several times, copyright is most easily understood as the sum of its parts: who has the right to copy a work. WIPO notes that copyright gives the creator both economic and moral rights to a work ("Copyright" n.d.). In the United States, these rights are delineated in Section 106 of Title 17 of the Code. Creators can reproduce works, make derivative works, and perform or display the work publicly. One question that sometimes comes up is the transferring of copyright. This is important for intellectual freedom because, as many publishers will tell you, it is often easier to secure international distribution if you have one place that manages copyright permissions around the globe. For example, even though I maintain the copyright to this book, my contract states that I give ALA permission to print, reproduce, and distribute the book around the world.

Even while retaining copyright there are exceptions to these rights in certain circumstances. WIPO outlines studies of these exceptions on their website: https://www.wipo.int/copyright/en/limitations/. Of particular interest are the studies on education, archives and libraries, and visual impairment exceptions. In the United States exceptions are outlined in Sections 107 to 111 of the Code. Briefly, Section 107 concerns fair use, 108 focuses on libraries and archives, 109 concerns the right of first sale, 110 has to do with performances and display of works, and 111 concerns cable broadcasting. For the purposes of this chapter, we will focus only on 107 and 108 and briefly on 109.

RIGHT OF FIRST SALE

One of the most important exceptions to copyright for libraries and used bookstores is the right of first sale. This exception allows the owner of a printed work to do what they like with it including allowing others to borrow it or sell it. As ALA notes on its resource page on the right of first sale, "Quite simply, first sale is what allows libraries to do what we do—lend books and materials to our patrons, the public" (ALA n.d.). Making hard copy books and other materials accessible would be impossible without this exception.

In the mid-2010s, there was concern that the right of first sale would be removed in the United States. Although the right was reaffirmed by the United States Supreme Court in 2013 for materials created abroad in the case *Kirtsaeng v. John Wiley & Sons, Inc.*, it was unclear how the justices would rule as the case made its way through the lower courts. As Jennifer Ferretti (2013, 273) states:

> The Opinion of the Court directly addresses arguments made by the respondent and those found in amicus briefs written in support of the respondent. The respondent argues that books manufactured overseas are not included within the phrase "lawfully made under this title" and that the Supreme Court has already favored this interpretation in Quality King. Regardless of the respondent's opinion, the Supreme Court

has ruled in favor of Kirtsaeng, which potentially protected future court cases against libraries and second market retailers.

(Note that the respondent in the case is the publisher John Wiley and Sons.)

It is important to note that digital files are not covered by the right of first sale as will be discussed in more detail below. This means that publishers are legally allowed to add digital rights management software to e-books, music, and other digital files to limit the number of times that they may be accessed. For libraries and other information institutions, this has profound budget and accessibility implications.

FAIR USE

Fair use is one of the most confusing and most important aspects of copyright law. Although lawyers may disagree, it is fair use that allows for much of the circulation of information and ideas. Fair use is an exception to copyright. Although it is often invoked, fair use is not always well understood.

Section 107 of the Copyright Code states:

> Notwithstanding the provisions of sections 106 and 106A, the fair use of a copyrighted work, including such use by reproduction in copies or phonorecords or by any other means specified by that section, for purposes such as criticism, comment, news reporting, teaching (including multiple copies for classroom use), scholarship, or research, is not an infringement of copyright. In determining whether the use made of a work in any particular case is a fair use the factors to be considered shall include—
>
> (1) the purpose and character of the use, including whether such use is of a commercial nature or is for nonprofit educational purposes;
> (2) the nature of the copyrighted work;
> (3) the amount and substantiality of the portion used in relation to the copyrighted work as a whole; and
> (4) the effect of the use upon the potential market for or value of the copyrighted work.
>
> The fact that a work is unpublished shall not itself bar a finding of fair use if such finding is made upon consideration of all the above factors (US Code, Title 17, Section 107).

These four factors—purpose, nature, amount, and effect—must all be balanced. One does not outweigh the other and all must be considered when applying fair use.

The first factor, purpose, refers to how a copyrighted work will be used. The law makes distinctions between for-profit and not-for-profit uses. For example, educational uses fit into this factor as a not-for-profit use of copyrighted material. The next factor, the nature of the work, is a bit more complicated but refers to the "characteristics and qualities" of the work (Crews 2020, 142). Crews notes that the law tends to be more lenient with the use of nonfiction works as they are "exactly the types of works for which fair use can have the most meaning" (Crews 2020, 143). This is because it is the distribution and access to nonfiction works that often lead to research and innovation in society.

The third factor, amount, refers to how much of a work is used. Again, fiction versus nonfiction books provides a good example for thinking about the nature and amount factors. Using one chapter of a fiction book constitutes a different type of use than using one chapter in a nonfiction book. You may capture an entire argument or all of the work of one author in an edited volume in a nonfiction book. A chapter in a fiction book may only give you a feel for the work. The fourth factor, effect, refers to what the impact of using the work will be on the creator regardless of the user's willingness or ability to pay. As Crews notes, that "effect" is closely linked to "purpose" but even in the area of education there are not hard and fast rules. "The hard reality is that even some educational uses have direct and adverse market consequences" (Crews 2020, 148). Fair use is governed by two sets of guidelines, neither of which is legally binding. The first is the National Commission on New Technological Uses of Copyright Works (CONTU) from 1976. The second set is from the 1997 Conference on Fair Use (CONFU), which failed to reach a consensus among stakeholders but did result in a set of guidelines for consultation.

An important distinction to understand when it comes to copyright is the difference between two definitions of the English word "free." Unlike some other languages, English uses "free" to mean *gratis* or at no monetary cost and also to mean *libre* or with no restriction. These are two very different concepts, and it is unfortunate that they are often conflated in the English language. The word "free" has profound implications for the open access movement (discussed more below) and its financial support models as more often than not it is concerned with providing information for free *gratis* rather than for free *libre*.

DIGITAL MILLENNIUM COPYRIGHT ACT OF 1998

It may be surprising that the 1976 law has not been revised in full. In 1997, President Bill Clinton convened CONFU to propose revisions to the law. The stakeholders could not agree on revisions—a response to the rise of the internet and digital media. Instead, several amendments were added to the 1976 law. For those interested in intellectual freedom, keep in mind that this is a truly reactionary law. In some respects, you can sense the panic that the internet engendered by looking at the entertainment industry. The Digital Millennium Copyright Act is a reactionary response to user power. It made digital files a separate category than other types of materials. One reason for this which is not discussed much is that copies of digital files are exact replicas. A quick example will explain why this matters for intellectual freedom. When you make a photocopy of a text or create a cassette mix tape, there is a loss of fidelity in the text or sound—the text is a bit blurred or the sound has scratches from the tape. This is not true of digital copies, which are usually lossless. The copy of a file is often a near perfect match with the original file. One can see why the entertainment industry in particular would be worried about this.

At its most basic, the Digital Millennium Copyright Act (DMCA) removed the fair use exception for digital files. As the *Intellectual Freedom Manual* notes, the DMCA made it "unlawful to circumvent digital protection mechanisms that block access to a work" (Russell 2021, 171). The DCMA is the law behind criminal suits for tampering with digital rights management. It is also the law that erected a *rentier* structure for digital files. A person or institution does not own the file but rents them from the purveyor. This is why Amazon was able to remove copies of George Orwell's *1984* from Kindle devices in 2009 (Stone 2009). People who have Kindles own the devices but not the book files that they purchase from

Amazon. The DMCA also removed the right of first sale, which has led to ongoing negotiations between libraries and publishers for access to e-books.

1998 COPYRIGHT TERM EXTENSION ACT

Here we encounter the importance of Mickey Mouse. Mickey Mouse first appeared to the public on November 18, 1928, in the cartoon *Steamboat Willie* (a short excerpt of which, for trademark reasons, can now be seen before many Disney projects). Mickey was scheduled to go into the public domain in 2003 (Crockett 2016). But, as this year approached, Disney started lobbying Congress to extend the copyright term. It is no coincidence that the act was named after Sonny Bono, who represented much of Los Angeles as the representative from the 44th district of California and who was a staunch proponent of copyright extension. The 1998 law extended copyright terms to life of the author plus seventy years. If a work was published before January 1, 1978, copyright was extended by twenty years for a total of ninety-five years. Mickey Mouse is now scheduled to enter the public domain on January 1, 2024.

This extension of copyright has led to the "orphan works" problem. As the *Intellectual Freedom Manual* notes, "because formal registration and renewal of copyright are no longer required, it can be difficult to find rights holders because there is no record of who to contact to ask permission. If a person cannot locate a rights holder for permission, they are likely to forgo use of the work" (Russell 2021, 171). This is important for intellectual freedom because in many respects it stifles creativity and the dissemination of new ideas and works. A negative example is useful here. Arthur Conan Doyle's early Sherlock Holmes short stories have been in the public domain for many years. From a creative point of view, this has led to an explosion of works featuring this character. A quick search on the Internet Movie Database (IMDB) provides the titles of 254 different movies and television shows—everything from 2010's *Tom and Jerry Meet Sherlock Holmes* to the 1940s Basil Rathbone movies. There is a modern-day Japanese TV series called *Miss Sherlock* and an Australian animated series from the 1980s. When it comes to books, there are innumerable editions of the early stories, from Dover Thrift's $8.00 paperbacks to the Folio Society's £40 illustrated editions. Not to mention the books inspired by Sherlock Holmes, including *A Study in Charlotte* by Brittany Cavallaro and *Mycroft Holmes* by Kareem Abdul-Jabbar and Anna Waterhouse.

Sherlock Holmes also provides an example of how copyright laws can stifle freedom of expression. The *Enola Holmes* book series by Nancy Springer which focuses on Sherlock's younger teenage sister also provides an interesting example. The first book of the series was made into a movie on Netflix in 2020. Sir Arthur Conan Doyle's estate sued Netflix (which had bought the rights to film the books), the author, her publisher, and the production company for the book's depiction of a "warm, respectful, and kind" Sherlock. To understand this lawsuit, it is important to note that ten Holmes stories published between 1923 and 1927 were still under copyright when the lawsuit was filed in 2020. These are the stories where Sherlock is depicted as "warm, respectful, and kind," whereas in the other public domain stories, he is depicted as "cold and critical." The lawsuit notes:

> Among other copied elements, the Springer novels make extensive infringing use of Conan Doyle's transformation of Holmes from cold and critical to warm, respectful and kind in his relationships. Springer places Enola Holmes at the center of the novels and has Holmes initially treat her coolly, then change to respond to her with warmth and kindness. In his copyright 1924 story, "The Three Garridebs," Conan Doyle created this new emotion and friendship in Sherlock Holmes. ("Sherlock—DocumentCloud" n.d., 8)

By this time, Springer had already written six Enola Holmes books, the first of which (*The Case of the Missing Marquess*) was published in 2006. Sir Arthur Conan Doyle died in 1930. Judge Richard Posner of the US Seventh Circuit dismissed the lawsuit with prejudice, but it is important to remember the time and finances that were required to respond in the first place (Flood 2020). In addition, the Conan Doyle Estate consists of eight people "all but one of whom are the beneficiaries of the will of Dame Jean Conan Doyle, the youngest child of Sir Arthur Conan Doyle. Most of the family are relations of Sir Arthur, by marriage or blood" (https://conandoyleestate.com/the-family). The estate's web page encourages creators to "work with the estate to maximize your potential" (https://conandoyleestate.com/licensing/trademarks-and-copyrights) and arguably to make sure that you don't get sued. Given this type of notice from the state, it is hard to argue with the idea that copyright term extensions have a chilling effect on intellectual freedom.

In general, visual art is protected by *droit moral*. As Jody Newmyer (1976, 40) notes in her article on art, libraries, and censorship, "the American public has historically had less tolerance for departure from orthodoxy in art than in printed material." Librarians and other information professionals should consult Kristin Pekoll's book (2019) to review practices that will protect art in public institutions.

ALTERNATIVES TO COPYRIGHT

Over the years, several alternatives to intellectual property law, particularly in general copyright, have developed. One is the open access movement. Readers are encouraged to consult other sources for more information but, briefly, open access is a method for making journals royalty-free. There are pros and cons to open access. As Peter Suber (2012) notes, it is compatible with copyright, print, and peer review. However, one of the primary effects of open access is that it transfers the cost of publication from the user and publisher to the author. This has both positive and negative consequences for knowledge circulation. The cost transfer means that users are able to more easily find and use works but, at the same time, pressure or requirements to publish open access can hinder some creators.

Another alternative is Creative Commons, which is actually an interpretation of the copyright law that provides easy-to-understand licensing alternatives that anyone can use. The history of Creative Commons demonstrates how stakeholders have grappled with some of the issues above. Creative Commons notes that "copyright licenses and tools forge a balance inside the traditional 'all rights reserved' setting that copyright law creates. Our tools give everyone from individual creators to large companies and institutions a simple, standardized way to grant copyright permissions to their creative work" (https://creativecommons.org/licenses). Each Creative Commons license has three layers, "the lawyer-readable legal code, the human-readable deed, and the machine-readable code."

There are alternatives to copyright that are simply illegal under current law. Sci-Hub, for example, has long been a target of scientific journal copyright holders. Library Genesis, a file-sharing network, is another service that provides access to paywalled information. Information professionals can be sympathetic to the need for such tools in this age of intranational and international wealth inequality while also holding to professional ethics that do not encourage their use. This can be difficult, especially in the United States under the current copyright law. With such lengthy copyright terms, it is difficult to fault those who look for alternatives that are outside the law.

COPYRIGHT AND INTELLECTUAL FREEDOM

As noted, at first glance copyright can seem tangential to intellectual freedom. It is, however, the air we are all swimming in. Intellectual property, and copyright law in particular, structure the creation and dissemination of information. When one looks around the globe, these can sometimes conflict with one another; copyright law in one country can be quite different from the law in other countries. However, the structure of copyright allows for the circulation of knowledge in society. It determines how people will legally exercise their right to intellectual freedom.

DISCUSSION QUESTIONS

- Are there certain types of information that should not be covered by copyright? How do you make that determination?
- How do you respond if a user asks how to use Sci-Hub?
- How do you balance the needs of patrons with the rights of copyright holders?

FURTHER READING

Albanese, Andrew. 2020. "Macmillan Abandons Library E-Book Embargo." PublishersWeekly.com. https://www.publishersweekly.com/pw/by-topic/industry-news/libraries/article/82715-macmillan-abandons-library-e-book-embargo.html.
   Although there are several examples, the controversy that ensued after the publisher Macmillan decided to embargo its new books in libraries provides a glimpse into the power of digital rights management and the lack of the right of first sale for digital files. After pressure, Macmillan decided not to place an embargo on new e-book titles. However, the threat of removal of access remains.

Creative Commons for Educators and Librarians. 2021. https://certificates.creativecommons.org/about/certificate-resources-cc-by/.
   This book is a remix of the Creative Commons certificate course content and is freely available on the Creative Commons website. It is published under the CC BY 4.0 licenses, which means the user can share and adapt with proper attribution.

Crews, Kenneth D. 2020. *Copyright Law for Librarians and Educators: Creative Strategies and Practical Solutions*. Chicago: American Library Association.
   Crews's frequently updated monograph is the standard text for copyright law in libraries and schools. It provides a wealth of information on how to understand copyright law.

Greshake, Bastian. 2017. "Looking into Pandora's Box: The Content of Sci-Hub and Its Usage." *F1000Research* 6 (April): 541. https://doi.org/10.12688/f1000research.11366.1.
   Greshake provides a history and overview of Sci-Hub, which he calls an example of "guerilla open access." Readers are also encouraged to follow updates on Sci-Hub and other similar services on their favorite news sources as the status of these resources changes quickly.

Heller, Michael A., and James Salzman. 2021. *Mine!: How the Hidden Rules of Ownership Control Our Lives*. New York: Knopf Doubleday Publishing Group.
   This accessible book on ownership provides an overview of the concept of property. Chapter 3, "I Reap What You Sow," focuses on copyright.

Knappenberger, Brian. 2014. *The Internet's Own Boy: The Story of Aaron Swartz*. Documentary.
> This documentary by Brian Knappenberger surveys the life of Aaron Swartz. Swartz, who died by suicide in 2013, was an internet activist who was being prosecuted by the United States government for downloading millions of files from JSTOR. The documentary is freely available on several platforms.

Moore, Adam D. 2013. "Concepts of Intellectual Freedom and Copyright." In *The Book: A Global History,* edited by Michael F. Suarez S. J. and H. R. Woudhuysen, 183-96. Oxford: Oxford University Press.
> This chapter in a one-volume encyclopedic history of the book provides an overview of the history and moral philosophy of intellectual property and copyright.

Suber, Peter. 2012. *Open Access*. Cambridge, MA: MIT Press. https://direct.mit.edu/books/book/3754/Open-Access.
> Suber, the director of the Harvard Office for Scholarly Communication, provides a concise overview of the open access movement. The book itself is published open access under a Creative Commons "By" license and is available on the MIT Press website.

United States Copyright Office. copyright.gov.
> Similar to the WIPO website, the US Copyright Office website provides many resources for understanding copyright in the United States. The office is part of the Library of Congress but this is regularly up for debate in Congress.

World Intellectual Property Organization. wipo.int.
> The WIPO website provides a wealth of information on intellectual property around the globe, including several primers on IP law. Readers are encouraged to review the organization's upcoming meetings to discover the latest discussion in international IP law and regulations.

REFERENCES

Albanese, Andrew. n.d. "Change at the Copyright Office." PublishersWeekly.Com. https://www.publishersweekly.com/pw/by-topic/digital/copyright/article/71885-change-at-the-copyright-office.html.

American Library Association. 2021. Code of Ethics. www.ifmanual.org/codeethics.

———. n.d. "LibGuides: Copyright for Libraries: First Sale Doctrine." https://libguides.ala.org/copyright/firstsale.

Association for Information Science and Technology. 1992. "ASIS&T Professional Guidelines." May 30, 1992. https://www.asist.org/about/asist-professional-guidelines/.

"Copyright." n.d. https://www.wipo.int/copyright/en/.

"Copyright Timeline: A History of Copyright in the United States." n.d. *Association of Research Libraries* (blog). https://www.arl.org/copyright-timeline/.

Crews, Kenneth D. 2020. *Copyright Law for Librarians and Educators: Creative Strategies and Practical Solutions*. Chicago: American Library Association.

Crockett, Zachary. 2016. "How Mickey Mouse Evades the Public Domain." *Priceonomics*, January 7, 2016. https://priceonomics.com/how-mickey-mouse-evades-the-public-domain/.

Davis, David D. 2019. "Noah Webster, America's First Copyright Lobbyist." SSRN Scholarly Paper ID 3399697. Rochester, NY: Social Science Research Network. https://papers.ssrn.com/abstract=3399697.

Ferretti, Jennifer A. 2013. "First Sale Decided: The Road to the *Kirtsaeng v. Wiley* Decision and What It Means for Libraries." *The Serials Librarian* 65 (3-4): 261-76. https://doi.org/10.1080/0361526X.2013.836464.

Flood, Alison. 2020. "Lawsuit over 'Warmer' Sherlock Depicted in Enola Holmes Dismissed." *The Guardian*, December 22, 2020. https://www.theguardian.com/books/2020/dec/22/lawsuit-copyright-warmer-sherlock-holmes-dismissed-enola-holmes.

Gilmer, Lois C. 1994. *Interlibrary Loan: Theory and Management*. Santa Barbara, CA: Libraries Unlimited, Inc.

Jacobs, Samuel. 2016. "The Effect of the 1886 Berne Convention on the US Copyright System's Treatment of Moral Rights and Copyright Term, and Where That Leaves Us Today." *Michigan Telecommunications and Technology Law Review* 23 (1): 169–90. https://repository.law.umich.edu/mttlr/vol23/iss1/5.

Newman, Robin, and Deborah Zemke. 2015. *The Case of the Missing Carrot Cake*. A Wilcox and Griswold Mystery. Berkeley, CA: Creston Books.

Newmyer, Jody. 1976. "Art, Libraries, and the Censor." *Library Quarterly* 46 (1): 38–53. www.jstor.org/stable/4306600.

Pekoll, Kristin. 2019. *Beyond Banned Books: Defending Intellectual Freedom throughout Your Library*. Chicago: American Library Association.

Russell, Carrie. 2021. "The Law Regarding Copyright." In *Intellectual Freedom Manual*, edited by Martin Garnar et al., 10th ed., 167–73. Chicago: American Library Association.

"Sherlock—DocumentCloud." n.d. https://www.documentcloud.org/documents/6956021-Sherlock.htm.

Stone, Brad. 2009. "Amazon Erases Orwell Books From Kindle." *The New York Times*, July 18, 2009. https://www.nytimes.com/2009/07/18/technology/companies/18amazon.html.

Suber, Peter. 2012. *Open Access*. Cambridge, MA: MIT Press. https://direct.mit.edu/books/book/3754/Open-Access.

"Trade Secrets." n.d. https://www.wipo.int/tradesecrets/en/index.html.

United Nations. 1948. "The Universal Declaration of Human Rights." www.un.org/en/documents/udhr/.

WIPO. n.d. "Standing Committee on Copyright and Related Rights (SCCR)." https://www.wipo.int/edocs/mdocs/copyright/en/sccr_41/sccr_41_1_prov.pdf.

CHAPTER 7

Intellectual Freedom and the Information Professions

INTELLECTUAL FREEDOM AS A PROFESSIONAL VALUE

In the early twenty-first century, supporting intellectual freedom remains a core value in librarianship and other information professions. The codes of ethics and professional guidelines of both the American Library Association (ALA) and the Association for Information Science and Technology (ASIS&T) include provisions for supporting intellectual freedom for all. This chapter will focus specifically on intellectual freedom and the information professions. It begins with an overview of the acceptance of intellectual freedom as a core value in librarianship and how this value has always been contested. It then provides an overview of professional values and discusses codes of ethics, as well as other guideline documents, including the Freedom to Read Statement, the Freedom to View Statement, and the Library Bill of Rights. Finally, the chapter ends with a discussion of intellectual freedom, neutrality, and social justice in librarianship and other information professions.

In 1876, when ALA was established, most librarians did not support intellectual freedom as a professional value. For example, as Evelyn Geller notes, librarians at the Boston Public Library followed ideas of moral censorship and improving the ethics and practices of their patrons. "The freedom to read as it had come to be perceived had little to do with the aspirations of the founders of the first public libraries . . . libraries were established in opposition not to censorship but to privilege" (Geller 1984, 11). Librarians at the time were especially vexed by the question of whether or not people should read fiction. Although we rarely think about it, when someone tells "fiction," this means that they are saying something that is not true. Is fiction good for one's moral development if it is not true? As we shall see throughout this chapter, questions of truth, its circulation and interpretation, and intellectual freedom have long been issues for librarians and other information professionals.

INTELLECTUAL FREEDOM, US LIBRARIANSHIP, AND THE LIBRARY BILL OF RIGHTS

Supporting intellectual freedom is strongly associated with professional librarianship (Knox 2014b). The adoption of freedom of expression and information as a human right and its subsequent integration in global librarianship in the mid-to-late twentieth century is discussed in chapter 2. This chapter will focus on how intellectual freedom was adopted by US librarianship in the early twentieth century. In *Forbidden Books in American Public Libraries, 1876-1939*, Geller traces the history of US librarianship's adoption of support for intellectual freedom through the lens of ideology. Geller, using the work of sociologist Talcott Parsons, defines ideology as "as a system of truth claims and values through which a group justifies its existence" (Geller 1984, xvi). More specifically, support for intellectual freedom allowed the budding profession of librarianship to claim its autonomy from other types of expertise.

As discussed above, Geller notes that when public libraries were first established in the nineteenth century, they were built on ideas of moral censorship and did not include popular novels in their collections. The first controversy in the 1880s over collection materials at Boston Public Library was over so-called "trashy" books. Interestingly, this led to the development of a children's department that would have its own separate collection and catalog so that children would not be exposed to problematic materials. These "trashy" books included Walt Whitman's *Leaves of Grass* and Gustave Flaubert's *Madame Bovary*. This is also the time that an ideology of neutrality began to develop in US librarianship. Librarians began to assert "their autonomy in the name of censorship. They used that value to demonstrate their professionalism on intellectual and ethical grounds—their superior judgment, or expertise, on harmful literature, and their greater commitment to the public good" (Geller 1984, 39). In other words, it was librarians who knew best which books would help or harm individual patrons. This was a neutrality based on exclusion. Eventually, naturalistic fiction became a legitimate form of literature, and such books were included in library collections. As Geller (1984, 199) writes, "literary masterpieces are never immoral—only 'unsuitable' for certain readers." That is, everyone should read them but only at the "right" time. The implicit norm of neutrality also changed from one of exclusion to one that focused on all sides of an issue.

Geller argues that libraries rarely collected controversial material after World War I. There were also new ideas about the public library, especially as an educational institution, which led to the idea that there should be open shelves for educational exploration and serendipity. The rise of Nazism in Germany during the 1930s meant that libraries had to reevaluate their stances on neutrality and propaganda. The Nazi threat made librarians less likely to want to be neutral. Did neutrality make sense given the times? Geller (1984, 172) also states that "critics of neutrality saw a false dichotomy between neutrality and advocacy." These critiques of neutrality would again arise in the 1970s and in the 2010s.

Although the Des Moines Public Library is often cited as the first library to adopt a Library Bill of Rights that, among other provisions, codified support for intellectual freedom, Joyce Latham (2009) notes in her article on Abe Korman that it was actually the Chicago Public Library that had the first Bill of Rights. According to Latham's research, during the 1930s, the Chicago Public Library board went further than any other library in its support for intellectual freedom. Latham argues this history is overlooked because the board supported left-wing/labor politics whereas both Geller and Louise Robbins's (discussed below) histories of intellectual freedom and librarianship focused on New Deal politics (Latham 2009, 289).

After the Des Moines Public Library established its Bill of Rights for a Free Public Library in 1938, ALA followed the model of both the Chicago Public Library and the Des Moines Public Library and adopted its own Library Bill of Rights (LBR) in 1939. In her follow-up to Geller's work, Louise Robbins notes that even though ALA had a policy, it did not provide structural or monetary support for it (Robbins 1996). In addition, most librarians did not follow the LBR and tended to underrepresent progressive positions in their collections. Librarians were not ready to accept intellectual freedom as a core value of the profession and "at this stage in the code's development, it was not accepted as defining professionally excerpted attitudes and behavior and, thus, failed to provide individual librarians with social support" (Robbins 1996, 26). It was not until the examination of the status of propaganda in the library during the anti-communism debates in the late 1940s and 1950s that librarians would accept intellectual freedom as a core value of the profession.

PROPAGANDA AND INTELLECTUAL FREEDOM

After the long debate over the status of fiction in the library, the status of propaganda once again defined the meaning and practices of librarianship. Although it often has a negative connotation, propaganda can be defined as information that individuals or organizations circulate in order to persuade others to a particular point of view (Saunders 2013, 311). ALA adopted a new version of the Library Bill of Rights in 1948 amid discussion of loyalty oaths and communism in the wider society. ALA's newly constituted Intellectual Freedom Committee opposed labeling propaganda, but the question of what to do with it always was and continues to be difficult to answer. Today, the terms "misinformation" and "disinformation" are often used rather than "propaganda" but the issues remain. What is the librarian's duty to point out information that is misleading to their patrons? Does information with a particular ideological or political bent need to be singled out? Although some argued that democratic societies depend on the availability of many points of view, as Robbins (1996, 55) notes, librarians still took their code of "the best books" to heart:

> Thus, although [librarians'] discourse was a discourse of inclusion and access, their actions generally were circumscribed by their tacit understanding of their community's limits. This contradiction grew out of librarians' shifting understanding of who they were and their desire for professional autonomy. As guardians of cultural values, they defended their autonomy by articulating their right to exclude or restrict access to materials, because they assumed they knew what reading material contributed to their patrons' "best personal development."

In 1951, former ALA President Ralph Ulveling's request that ALA's Statement on Labeling include a provision for the separation of communist propaganda revealed a lack of consensus regarding intellectual freedom in the association (Robbins 1993). Although most librarians supported free access to materials, in practice they segregated controversial material (Lowenthal 1959; Busha 1972). To combat this propensity, ALA's Intellectual Freedom Committee instituted several workshops designed to educate librarians on the principle of intellectual freedom. In the end, Robbins (1996, 66) argues that debates over labeling propaganda and taking loyalty oaths demonstrate ideological conflicts within librarianship and also show how ideology is mediated through conflict. As has been seen throughout this book, current debates of ideological tensions between social justice and intellectual freedom define librarianship and other information professions today.

From the early 1950s to 1969, ALA increased structural support for intellectual freedom, and the profession enhanced its prestige and authority through its relations to considering freedom to read as a democratic ideal. The so-called Fiske Report (1959) by Marjorie Fiske Lowenthal highlighted the prevalence of self-censorship as a means to avoid controversy among librarians (Collier 2010). According to Robbins (1996, 100),

> [The report] emphasized the vulnerable position of librarians in their communities, their sense of isolation and subordination as professionals, and their uncertainty about their autonomy in matters of book selection. The "free-floating anxiety" and the atmosphere of repression that caused "timid" librarians to avoid external pressures by practicing self-censorship long had been described in the library literature.

Lowenthal's report demonstrated the difficulty of praxis, which here might be understood as putting ideology into practice.

SELECTION AND CENSORSHIP

Along with supporting intellectual freedom, the question of how to select books was also of primary importance. Lester Asheim's "Not Censorship but Selection" (1953) became one of the defining articles of the profession. The classic piece asks: "What is the difference between not buying an item to censor and not buying it due to selection?" First, Asheim takes what might be called the modernist-agnostic view of reading effects wherein one cannot know what the particular individual effect of being exposed to knowledge might be (Knox 2014a). Then Asheim (1953, 5) states the difference between selection and censorship very clearly:

> For to the selector, the important thing is to find reasons to keep the book. Given such a guiding principle, the selector looks for values, for strengths, for virtues which will over shadow [sic] minor objections. For the censor, on the other hand, the important thing is to find reasons to reject the book; his guiding principle leads him to seek out the objectionable features, the weaknesses, the possibilities for misinterpretation. The positive selector asks what the reaction of a rational intelligent adult would be to the content of the work; the censor fears for the results on the weak, the warped, and the irrational.

It is not an exaggeration to say that Asheim's principles have provided a guide for understanding the work of librarianship for the past seventy years. Although censorship is often understood as a response to a failing of the work itself, Asheim posits that censorship is an issue of criteria external, rather than internal, to the work. That is, censorship is about interpretation. It is not coincidental that ALA adopted the Freedom to Read (FTR) Statement in 1953. Its seven propositions include the following:

> Publishers, librarians, and booksellers do not need to endorse every idea or presentation they make available. It would conflict with the public interest for them to establish their own political, moral, or aesthetic views as a standard for determining what should be published or circulated. (ALA 2004)

The statement has been reaffirmed several times, most recently in 2004.

Along with increased structural support from ALA, the problem of racial integration of libraries was a major point of contention within the profession in the 1950s and 1960s. (This will be discussed more below in the section on neutrality.) Robbins also notes that the LBR "provided the social support needed to encourage conformity with professional values" (1996, 124) even in the midst of continued self-censorship. The LBR and the FTR statements (and eventually the Freedom to View Statement) became a part of library ideology.

Robbins (1996, 2) also argues that the ideology of librarianship is actually quite conservative (in the classic sense of the term) as support for intellectual freedom is in keeping with the maintenance of pluralist ideology. One of Robbins's ideas is that reading is one of the most important parts of librarianship: "Librarians are in the peculiar position of saying that reading matters, that it entails risks, and, at the same time, resisting any restrictions on access to books and other library materials" (Robbins 1996, 156). As seen throughout this book, librarianship in fact has a contradictory mission: providing access to information while at the same time uplifting the importance of reading.

INTELLECTUAL FREEDOM AND SOCIETAL CHANGE

Many issues that continue to roil librarianship and other information professionals began during the civil rights movement of the 1950s and 60s and continued through the other empowerment movements of the mid-to-late twentieth century. In her history of intellectual freedom and librarianship from 1967 to 1974, Toni Samek (2001) traces the rise of social responsibility as a major movement in US librarianship. This shift is related to previous controversies regarding "the best reading" or reading that will improve one's character but has a different foundation and impact on the profession.

Interestingly, the foundation for this shift is based not in propaganda wars but in the rise of the alternative press. In the 1960s the Radical Research Center established the Alternative Press Index (API). At the time indexes were the primary mechanism for providing access to periodical materials. The API was not a professional index, and professional response to it was mixed (Samek 2001, 26), but it was the only method for providing access to topics covered by the alternative press in the United States.

The framework of neutrality that had its foundations in collecting all sides of arguments, which was the ideological basis of the LBR, received increased criticism in the 1960s when librarians became concerned that neutrality was simply a shield for prejudice. This was often discussed in terms of the idea that collections should be balanced. Despite this, librarians were often reluctant to collect materials from the alternative press because those materials themselves were not seen as being neutral.

The years 1967–1969 were pivotal for US librarianship, especially in the American Library Association, and thus important for understanding the theoretical frameworks for intellectual freedom and social justice in the late twentieth and early twenty-first centuries. ALA established two committees to discuss changes to the profession. The first was the Activities Committee on New Directions (ACONDA), and the second was the Ad Hoc Activities Committee on New Directions (ANACONDA). "New directions" operated as a catchall for social change, social justice, and social responsibilities. Douglas Raber (2007) notes that the ACONDA developed six priorities for ALA: (1) social responsibilities, (2) manpower, (3) intellectual freedom, (4) legislation, (5) planning research and development, and (6) democratization and reorganization. These committees also offered two different definitions of social responsibility. The first, more traditional one focused on reflecting when all sides of an issue are collected but are not promoted. The other was an activist interpretation that focused on how librarianship contributed to social welfare (Samek 2001, 78). The Office for Intellectual Freedom, with Judith Krug as its first director, was also established during this time in 1967.

These recommendations eventually led to the decentralization of ALA and the establishment of "mission-oriented action units" (Samek 2001, 120). David Berninghausen, a former chair of the Intellectual Freedom Committee, was concerned that neutrality was becoming less salient to librarianship and worked to reaffirm its place as a core value by idealized collections. *Library Journal* published Berninghausen's opinion piece and nineteen responses between 1972 and 1973. Berninghausen argued that if the activist definition of social responsibility took hold librarians would not be free to make policy decisions for their communities without government or association interference. They would have to adhere to a particular partisan line." The ALA would take partisan positions on substantive issues unrelated to librarianship and would decide which books should be in libraries and which should be banned. The publications on the list above would be judged as good or bad for the general public, and these and other titles would get a stamp of approval or disapproval" (Berninghausen 1972, 3680). E. J. Josey's (1973, 32) response included the following observation:

> The trouble with Berninghausen's rejection of social responsibility is that it would permit just such studies . . . to be published without any attempt on the part of the librarians to place before a uniformed and unsuspecting public views which challenge those advocated by those by design or fortuity are able to reach the presses first.

That is, librarians would not be able to ensure that misinformation and disinformation is widely circulated. Throughout his essay, Josey makes an argument for intersectionality in understanding social identity.

Although most of the responses published in *Library Journal* critiqued Berninghausen's position, Samek notes that many librarians found Berninghausen persuasive because "much of the social responsibility activity resulted from ideological stands, because of their traditional reluctance to abandon a 'neutral' position, and because of their fear of potential social, financial and legal consequences of ALA involvement in non-library matters" (Samek 2001, 139). Although ALA established the Social Responsibilities Round Table, Samek argues that its mission is "smothered" by other overlapping round tables. However, in the end, as Samek states, librarians cannot avoid social issues.

INTELLECTUAL FREEDOM AND THE POST-CIVIL RIGHTS ERA

One of the most notorious incidents in US librarianship concerning freedom of expression and intellectual freedom was the screening of *The Speaker . . . A Film about Freedom* in 1977. This movie was commissioned and produced by the Intellectual Freedom Committee (IFC) and was immediately met with controversy. This movie about a high school that invited a racist professor to speak, which then leads to controversy in the community, was first pulled from the conference schedule but ultimately screened.

A 45-minute discussion followed the screening. Reactions were decidedly mixed and the debate was bitter. Council member E. J. Josey, cofounder of the Black Caucus of the American Library Association and a future ALA president, warned of alienating Black ALA members "if you continue to support that goddamned film." On the other hand, IFC member Ella Yates said, "I can personally accept its release with ALA's imprimatur affixed with greater pride than I could have accepted a replay of our professional performance in discussion on Sunday evening." *The Speaker* has fractured friendships and professional relationships since that day in Detroit (Jones 2014).

ALA rescreened the film at its annual conference in 2014 and it was again met with controversy. Robert Wedgeworth, ALA executive director during the screening, noted during a panel on the film "I've never spoken publicly about *The Speaker* . . . even my friends were reluctant to discuss it with me. It was a dream turned nightmare" (Morehart and Eberhart 2014). Readers are encouraged to review ALA's full archive of materials on both the 1977 and 2014 screenings of the film (https://www.ala.org/tools/atoz/speaker).

In the early 1980s the American Booksellers Association invited the director of the Office for Intellectual Freedom, Judith Krug, to work on a new project, Banned Books Week. Now organized by a coalition of sponsors, Banned Books Week celebrates the freedom to read every year during the last week of September. The coalition of fourteen organizations includes the American Society of Journalists and Authors, the Authors Guild, the Foundation for Individual Rights and Expression (FIRE), the National Coalition Against Censorship (NCAC, on whose board I currently serve), the National Council of Teachers of English (NCTE), PEN America, and the People for the American Way Foundation.

In 1990, ALA adopted the Freedom to View Statement (ALA 2006). Although not as well-known as the Freedom to Read Statement, it provides five principles to guide librarians when selecting audiovisual materials. For example, the fourth principle affirms the principle "to provide a diversity of viewpoints without the constraint of labeling or prejudging film, video, or other audiovisual materials on the basis of the moral, religious, or political beliefs of the producer or filmmaker or on the basis of controversial content." In addition, ALA developed and adopted a variety of interpretations of the Library Bill of Rights during the 1990s and 2000s. These include "User-Initiated Exhibits, Displays, and Bulletin Boards" and "Services to People with Disabilities." Readers are encouraged to review the full list of interpretations (https://www.ala.org/advocacy/intfreedom/librarybill/interpretations). Also, in response to requests from librarians around the world, in 1997 the International Federation of Library Associations and Institutions committee was dedicated to intellectual freedom and founded the Advisory Committee on Freedom of Access to Information and Freedom of Expression.

PROFESSIONAL VALUES AND ETHICS

The concepts of morals, values, and ethics were introduced in chapter 1; to review briefly, morals are a "a set of mores, customs, and traditions that may have been derived from social practice or from religious guidance" (Koehler 2003, 99). Values are a subset of morals that are "enduring beliefs," whereas ethics are the application of those values to various situations. In *Our Enduring Values Revisited*, Michael Gorman (2015) focuses on the guiding fundamental values of librarianship. Intellectual freedom is one of these core values, along with stewardship, service, rationalism, literacy and learning, equity of access to recorded knowledge and information, privacy, democracy, and the greater good (Gorman 2015, 35–37). Gorman states that "intellectual freedom begins with opposition to censorship of books and other library materials" and is "connected to the librarian's duty to make all library materials available to everyone" (110). He also offers a particular definition of censorship: "a censor as someone who does not want you to know or read what he knows or has read" (117).

It is significant that Gorman does not include neutrality as a key value of librarianship. As discussed above, for many years, neutrality was seen as a key professional value in librarianship. However, as Scott and Saunders (2021) found in their article on public librarians and librarianship, this value is not held as strongly as it once was. In many respects, "neutrality" is difficult to define, but Scott and Saunders found that the most common definition among the librarians they surveyed was "being objective in providing information" (Scott and Saunders 2021, 114).

Neutrality was and continues to be a contested value in librarianship. As Robert Wengert (2001) noted, "saying censorship is wrong is not a neutral position—libraries have taken a stand." The contested nature of neutrality can be seen in many spaces in librarianship and other information professions. For example, artificial intelligence scholar Timnit Gebru was forced out of Google when she asked for permission to publish a paper on the risks of its technology. Although Google seems to acknowledge that its algorithmic technologies are not neutral, the company seems to be pushing toward neutrality (Hao 2020). Many, however, argue that neutrality does not exist. As Jenna Freedman, the reference and zine librarian at Barnard College, once said, "you can be non-judgmental but not neutral because you are always making a choice." Deciding to do nothing is, in fact, a choice for the status quo.

In a talk I gave at the 2018 ALA Midwinter Presidential Forum, I asked the following question:

> Does not supporting the Black Lives Matter movement make the library neutral? My answer was no. Choosing not to support the movement means you have *made a decision* and making a decision is never neutral. These choices not to support a movement can mean that a library will not be embroiled in controversy but that does not mean that a choice has been made. One must also consider at what cost these choices are made and for whom. For example, if you have a Black History Month display then the library has already stated that, in fact, Black Lives Matter. Those people being celebrated were the black lives matter of their time. As Stephen Joyce [2008, 52] notes, neutrality is a form of fence sitting, a form of silence [emphasis in original]. (Carlton 2018)

In other information professions such as archives, records management, and information systems, the importance of intellectual freedom fluctuates. Archivists, for example, do not mention intellectual freedom in their core values statement and code of ethics. Those documents do, however, discuss access and use of records, stating that archivists should promote and provide the widest possible accessibility of materials, while respecting legal and ethical access restrictions, including public statutes, cultural protections, donor contracts, and privacy requirements. Although access may be justifiably limited in some instances, archivists still seek to foster open access and unrestricted use as broadly as possible (Society of American Archivists n.d.). The professional ethics guidelines of the Special Library Association also do not include intellectual freedom but focus on professionalism and good faith in professional practice (Special Libraries Association n.d.). As noted previously, the ASIS&T guidelines for ethics begin with access (ASIS&T 1992).

CODES OF ETHICS

The values of a profession are embedded in their codes of ethics. These codes serve many different purposes; one of the most important purposes is that they, in many respects, establish professions. As Geller (1984) discusses, it is impossible to be a professional if the role does not have a code of ethics that members of the profession hold as a standard. When ALA created its

Code of Ethics in 1939, this was the last step in the six-decade project to professionalize librarianship. Since that time, securing commitment to the profession's ethical values as delineated in the Code of Ethics has been the major focus of library science programs. Often one can understand what a particular profession strives toward by reading through its code of ethics and reviewing how these are incorporated into professional training.

Codes of ethics illuminate the professional's obligations on several different levels. First, there are obligations to individuals. As a professional, you have certain responsibilities to others, including respect and providing the best level of service. Next, codes of ethics delineate obligations to the profession. In this case, what do you owe your fellow librarians or information professionals, and what do they owe to you and others who are in the profession? Even though it is one of the least analyzed and discussed of the code's articles, the ALA Code of Ethics states: "we treat co-workers and other colleagues with respect, fairness, and good faith, and advocate conditions of employment that safeguard the rights and welfare of all employees of our institutions." In addition, the Code of Ethics also states: "we strive for excellence in the profession by maintaining and enhancing our own knowledge and skills, by encouraging the professional development of coworkers, and by fostering the aspirations of potential members of the profession." The idea that you owe yourself continuing education and professional development is an important consideration throughout your career.

Next there are obligations to the organization or institution. As a professional, you are encouraged to understand your institution or organization's mission statement and how these might affect your role as an information professional. It's important to know that some institutions may have missions that are at odds with the core values of librarianship and consider how you might make decisions in situations where there are conflicts. Finally, codes of ethics include obligations to society. As a professional, you are expected to contribute and make society as a whole better. (Interestingly, the ASIS&T professional guidelines name each of these obligations in turn.)

MOVING FORWARD

Intellectual freedom remains a contested value in librarianship even as it remains a prominent principle in codes of ethics in the United States and around the world. During the past decade or so, the question of how to integrate social justice and intellectual freedom has come to the forefront. The critical librarianship movement, and #critlib in particular, have argued that intellectual freedom can lead to harm, especially to people who are members of underrepresented and marginalized populations. The rise of misinformation and disinformation has made the argument against supporting intellectual freedom more attractive. In practice it is helpful to consider Jenna Freedman's admonition that, when it comes to intellectual freedom and collections, "strive to achieve representation—not balance."

However, with the increase in laws that oppose social justice, diversity, and inclusion in society and the rising numbers of book challenges in the United States—and also in the recent Russian and Chinese government crackdowns on dissenters and the press—it is easier to see how librarians must continue to support intellectual freedom for all. The restriction of expression tends to consolidate power into the hands of a few.

It is helpful to be guided by the history discussed above and consider why librarianship chose to support intellectual freedom as a principle. The words of Miriam Matthews (1905-2003), who was the first Black professional librarian who was hired by the Los Angeles Public Library (LAPL) system, are significant. Along with her work at the LAPL, she also served as the chair of the California Library Association's Committee for Intellectual Freedom during the tumultuous time of 1946-1948. The following is from her oral history transcript from 1977:

> I'm still against all forms of censorship. Even though some progress has been made, it still exists. It hardly seems possible that John Beecher, a college professor who is a descendant of Henry Ward Beecher, has just been reinstated at California State, San Francisco, along with several of his colleagues, after being discharged more than twenty-five years ago for refusing to sign a loyalty oath just to prove they were loyal Americans. It took an act of the California legislature to bring this about belatedly. Much of today's censorship involves books with strong language, which shocks individuals who cannot tell the difference between books which have literary merit and a social purpose, and those which are simply trash. There are these strange people who don't really read books regularly, so they pick up something that's modern, and maybe the last book they read was way back in school some twenty or thirty or fifty years ago. They may be a little shocked by the language, but what they do is take the sentence or the paragraph out of context. And if you read the whole book, you see that the author is giving a slice of a certain kind of life and he's describing it as it is. (Black Women Oral History Project, Interviews, 1976-1981)

Fifty years later there are still many threats to intellectual freedom, and librarians and other information professionals must remain vigilant.

DISCUSSION QUESTIONS

- What role do libraries play in intellectual freedom?
- What are some unique intellectual freedom issues that you might encounter in different information institutions?
- What resources might you use when you encounter these issues?

FURTHER READING

Burgess, John T. F. 2016. "Reconciling Social Responsibility and Neutrality in LIS Professional Ethics: A Virtue Ethics Approach." In *Information Cultures in the Digital Age: A Festschrift in Honor of Rafael Capurro*, edited by Jared Bielby and Matt Kelly. New York: Springer.
Burgess, my fellow editor of *Foundations of Information Ethics*, wrestles with one of the most vexing problems in librarianship: how to maintain both social justice and intellectual freedom as core values for the profession.

Gibson, Amelia N., Renate Chancellor, Nicole A. Cooke, Sarah Park Dahlen, Beth Patin, and Yasmeen Shorish. 2020. "Struggling to Breathe: COVID-19, Protest and the LIS Response." Preprint. *Equality, Diversity and Inclusion: An International Journal*. https://scholarcommons.sc.edu/cgi/viewcontent.cgi?article=1295&context=libsci_facpub.
This article by six library and information science professors discusses core professional values for library and information science in the wake of the COVID-19 pandemic and the murders of George Floyd, Breonna Taylor, and others.

LaRue, James. 2007. *The New Inquisition: Understanding and Managing Intellectual Freedom Challenges*. Westport, CT: Libraries Unlimited.

> LaRue is a former director of ALA's Office for Intellectual Freedom. His book discusses his experiences with book challenges when he was a library director. It also provides examples of how to respond to these challenges, including letters written to challengers themselves.

Nye, Valerie, editor. 2020. *Intellectual Freedom Stories from a Shifting Landscape*. Chicago: American Library Association.

> Materials challenges can be extremely isolating for library and school staff. Nye's edited volume (as well as its previous version, *True Stories of Censorship Battles in America's Libraries*—also published by ALA) gives library workers a forum to share their stories with others.

Oltmann, Shannon M. 2019. *Practicing Intellectual Freedom in Libraries*. Santa Barbara, CA: ABC-CLIO.

> This book by my fellow Mapping Information Access research team member provides both a strong theoretical foundation for understanding intellectual freedom and practical answers for implementing policy in public libraries.

Pekoll, Kristin. 2019. *Beyond Banned Books: Defending Intellectual Freedom throughout Your Library*. Chicago: American Library Association.

> Written by the former assistant director of ALA's Office for Intellectual Freedom, this book provides practical solutions for supporting intellectual freedom in a variety of contexts, including art displays and social media.

Schrader, A. M. 1997. "Why You Can't Censorproof Your Public Library." *PLQ* 16 (1): 3–29.

> Even twenty-five years later, the message of this article remains relevant—trying to censorproof your library is futile.

REFERENCES

American Library Association. 2004. Freedom to Read Statement. www.ala.org/offices/oif/statementspols/ftrstatement/freedomreadstatement.

———. 2006. Freedom to View Statement. Text. Round Tables. September 29, 2006. www.ala.org/rt/vrt/professionalresources/vrtresources/freedomtoview.

Asheim, L. 1953. "Not Censorship but Selection." *Wilson Library Bulletin* 28 (1): 63–67.

Association for Information Science and Technology. 1992. "ASIS&T Professional Guidelines." May 30, 1992. https://www.asist.org/about/asist-professional-guidelines/.

Berninghausen, David K. 1972. "Antithesis in Librarianship: Social Responsibility vs. The Library Bill of Rights." *Undefined*. https://www.semanticscholar.org/paper/Antithesis-in-Librarianship%3A-Social-Responsibility-Berninghausen/dd6fe9a3b45cfa439dab54224dcdc45215722443.

Black Women Oral History Project. Interviews, 1976–1981. Miriam Matthews. OH-31. Schlesinger Library on the History of Women in America Institution, Radcliffe Institute, Harvard University, Cambridge, MA. Page (seq. 72). https://iiif.lib.harvard.edu/manifests/view/drs:45173973$72i.

Busha, Charles H. 1972. "Intellectual Freedom and Censorship: The Climate of Opinion in Midwestern Public Libraries." *Library Quarterly* 42 (3): 283–301. www.jstor.org.proxy.libraries.rutgers.edu/stable/4306179.

Carlton, Amy. 2018. "Are Libraries Neutral?" *American Libraries,* February 12, 2018. https://americanlibrariesmagazine.org/blogs/the-scoop/are-libraries-neutral/.

Collier, Ellie. 2010. "The Fiske Report." *In the Library with the Lead Pipe* (blog), June 23, 2010. www.inthelibrarywiththeleadpipe.org/2010/the-fiske-report/.

Geller, Evelyn. 1984. *Forbidden Books in American Public Libraries, 1876–1939: A Study in Cultural Change*. Westport, CT: Greenwood Press.

Gorman, Michael. 2015. *Our Enduring Values Revisited: Librarianship in an Ever-Changing World*. Chicago: American Library Association. http://public.ebookcentral.proquest.com/choice/publicfullrecord.aspx?p=2068198.

Hao, Karen. 2020. "We Read the Paper That Forced Timnit Gebru out of Google. Here's What It Says." *MIT Technology Review,* December 4, 2020. https://www.technologyreview.com/2020/12/04/1013294/google-ai-ethics-research-paper-forced-out-timnit-gebru/.

Jones, Barbara M. 2014. "The Speaker Controversy in the 21st Century." *American Libraries* (blog), May 29, 2014. https://americanlibrariesmagazine.org/blogs/the-scoop/the-speaker-controversy-in-the-21st-century/.

Josey, E. J. 1973. "Social Responsibility and the Library Bill of Rights: The Berninghausen Debate [Response]." *Library Journal* 98: 32-33.

Joyce, Stephen. 2008. "A Few Gates Redux: An Examination of the Social Responsibilities Debate in the Early 1970s and 1990s." In *Questioning Library Neutrality*, edited by Alison Lewis, 33-66. Duluth, MN: Library Juice Press, LLC.

Knox, Emily J. M. 2014a. "Intellectual Freedom and the Agnostic-Postmodern View of Reading Effects." *Library Trends* 63 (1): 11-26.

———. 2014b. "Supporting Intellectual Freedom: Symbolic Capital and Practical Philosophy in Librarianship." *Library Quarterly* 84 (1): 1-14.

Koehler, Wallace. 2003. "Professional Values and Ethics as Defined by 'The LIS Discipline.'" *Journal of Education for Library and Information Science* 44 (2): 99-119. https://doi.org/10.2307/40323926.

Latham, J. M. 2009. "Wheat and Chaff: Carl Roden, Abe Korman, and the Definitions of Intellectual Freedom in the Chicago Public Library." *Libraries and the Cultural Record* 44 (3): 279-98.

Lowenthal, Marjorie Fiske. 1959. *Book Selection and Censorship: A Study of School and Public Libraries in California*. Berkeley, CA: University of California Press.

Morehart, Phil, and George M. Eberhart. 2014. "Resurrecting the Speaker." *American Libraries,* July 1, 2014. http://americanlibrariesmagazine.org/blogs/the-scoop/resurrecting-the-speaker/.

Raber, Douglas. 2007. "ACONDA and ANACONDA: Social Change, Social Responsibility, and Librarianship." *Library Trends* 55 (3): 675-97. https://doi.org/10.1353/lib.2007.0020.

Robbins, Louise S. 1993. "Segregating Propaganda in American Libraries: Ralph Ulveling Confronts the Intellectual Freedom Committee." *Library Quarterly* 63 (2): 143-65. https://doi.org/10.1086/602556.

———. 1996. *Censorship and the American Library: The American Library Association's Response to Threats to Intellectual Freedom, 1939-1969*. Westport, CT: Greenwood Press.

Society of American Archivists. n.d. "Core Values Statement and Code of Ethics." https://www2.archivists.org/statements/saa-core-values-statement-and-code-of-ethics.

Samek, Toni. 2001. *Intellectual Freedom and Social Responsibility in American Librarianship: 1967-1974*. Jefferson, NC: McFarland.

Saunders, Laura. 2013. "Information as Weapon: Propaganda, Politics, and the Role of the Library." In *Imagine, Innovate, Inspire: The Proceedings of the ACRL 2013 Conference*, 4: 309-18.

Scott, Dani, and Laura Saunders. 2021. "Neutrality in Public Libraries: How Are We Defining One of Our Core Values?" *Journal of Librarianship and Information Science* 53 (1): 153-66. https://doi.org/10.1177/0961000620935501.

Special Libraries Association. n.d. "Professional Ethics Guidelines." https://www.sla.org/about-sla/competencies/sla-professional-ethics-guidelines/.

Wengert, R. G. 2001. "Some Ethical Aspects of Being an Information Professional." *Library Trends* 49 (3): 486-509.

CHAPTER 8

Current and Future Issues in Intellectual Freedom

WHERE WE ARE NOW AND WHERE WE MIGHT BE

One of the more interesting aspects of studying intellectual freedom is that the landscape can change quickly. Infringements to intellectual freedom and continuing support for it as a human right are often subject to societal and political forces that can change on a daily basis. The topics below are not meant to be exhaustive but to give the reader a sense of where current and future challenges lie. These are areas for deeper research and analysis.

The topics begin online and then move offline but are not arranged according to any perceived importance of the topic. Unlike the previous chapters, a list of recommendations for further reading is given for each issue immediately following the summary that provides a variety of points of view. Readers will note that many of the references and suggested readings are news articles or reports from non-governmental organizations. This is often because the topic is fast moving and scholarly or a book-length analysis does not yet exist.

INTERNET FILTERING AND FIREWALLS

On the international level, internet filters and/or firewalls are often used by repressive governments to ensure that citizens do not have access to certain types of information. For example, Iran filtered its internet prior to its elections in 2022 (Freedom House 2021). Although it uses different technology, China employs the "Great Firewall" to keep information from circulating among its citizens (Chandel et al. 2019). On a more local level in the United States, I have written extensively on internet filtering elsewhere with the Mapping Information Access team (https://mappinginfoaccess.org). Although the use of filters across the internet is now considered standard, filtering is often a tool of the powerful. In our research, the Mapping Information Access team has focused on the use of the publicly subsidized e-rate to encourage public institutions to employ filters on their computers. These filters are often poorly structured and block information that they should allow. Also, the filters are often used as human or classroom management tools: they keep kids off of social media in the classroom or keep adults from watching pornography in the public library. Internet filters are tools of censorship. They can be deployed with sensitivity and awareness, but often they are not.

Further Reading

Dellinger, Hannah. 2021. "'It Needs to Be Accessible by All': Katy ISD Blocks LGBTQ+ Resources, Suicide Prevention Website." *Houston Chronicle,* November 24, 2021. https://www.houstonchronicle.com/news/houston-texas/education/article/Katy-ISD-blocks-LGBTQ-resources-suicide-16647274.php.

    This news article demonstrates how internet filtering is used to block access to what might be called "difficult knowledge." As Dellinger notes, the Katy (TX) Independent School District is using their filter to overblock websites. Many of the websites described should be whitelisted in the district's filter.

Houghton, Sarah. 2010. "Chapter 4: Internet Filtering." *Library Technology Reports* 46 (8): 25–33.

    Houghton provides a comprehensive overview of the problems of internet filtering. This reading is highly recommended for anyone who wants to have a better understanding of how and why internet filtering is a threat to intellectual freedom.

Peterson, Chris, Shannon M. Oltmann, and Emily J. M. Knox. 2017. "The Inconsistent Work of Web Filters: Mapping Information Access in Alabama Public Schools and Libraries." *International Journal of Communication* 11: 4583–4609.

    The Mapping Information Access research team provides an in-depth overview of filtering in one state. This article gives a scholarly analysis of how internet filters are employed in Alabama public institutions.

Stoycheff, Elizabeth, G. Scott Burgess, and Maria Clara Martucci. 2020. "Online Censorship and Digital Surveillance: The Relationship between Suppression Technologies and Democratization across Countries." *Information, Communication and Society* 23 (4): 474–90. https://doi.org/10.1080/1369118X.2018.1518472.

    Stoycheff, Burgess, and Martucci provide a cross-country analysis of how governments censor the internet. They are particularly interested in the link between internet censorship and democratization movements around the globe. As they note, "surveillance, in particular, is detrimental because it is associated with lack of government transparency that, if left unchecked, can erode democratic efforts by making censorship more effective and weakening collective action."

SECTION 230

Although Section 230 is a statute in the US Communications Decency Act, it has worldwide implications for freedom of expression and intellectual freedom. Section 230 provides so-called "safe harbor" for online companies so that they are not legally responsible for information posted on their websites. This means that individuals cannot hold communications platforms liable for harm that derives from material that they publish. Tech companies, most famously Facebook/Meta, are calling for increased regulation for their platforms. Rather than taking on the burden of regulating expression on their private platforms, tech companies would prefer to put the development of rules and laws in the hands of the government. As always, the questions are: Who will benefit from this increased regulation? Will this regulation actually lead to a reduction of harassment, bullying, and harmful expression online? Who will make these decisions? Because many of the global tech giants are US companies, any changes to Section 230 will have global consequences.

Further Reading

Electronic Frontier Foundation. n.d. "Section 230 of the Communications Decency Act." https://www.eff.org/issues/cda230.

> The Electronic Frontier Foundation, a not-for-profit organization dedicated to "defending civil liberties in a digital world" provides many primers on a host of topics related to the internet. This is a basic introduction to Section 230 of the Communications Decency Act.

Meta (Facebook), and Monika Bickert. 2020. "Charting a Way Forward: Online Content Regulation." https://about.fb.com/wp-content/uploads/2020/02/Charting-A-Way-Forward_Online-Content-Regulation-White-Paper-1.pdf.

> This white paper delineates Meta's (i.e., Facebook's) legislative goals for Section 230. Monica Bickert is Meta's vice president for content policy. (As of the publication of this book, Meta controls many subsidiaries, including Facebook, Instagram, Messenger, WhatsApp, and Oculus.)

Villasenor, Maya. 2020. "Revisiting Section 230: The Implications Are International." Council on Foreign Relations. November 16, 2020. https://www.cfr.org/blog/revisiting-section-230-implications-are-international.

> At the time this article was published, Villasenor was an intern at the Council on Foreign Relations, a nonpartisan think tank. This article describes how changes to Section 230 affect global information access.

FOSTA/SESTA

The Fight Online Sex Trafficking Act (FOSTA) was passed in the US House of Representatives, and the Stop Enabling Sex Traffickers Act (SESTA) was the Senate bill. These were signed into law by former President Donald Trump in 2018. As with many laws that target online communication, the law on sex trafficking is extremely broad and has widespread implications. Although FOSTA and SESTA were meant to address the crime of sex trafficking, they accomplished this by targeting Section 230 of the Communications Decency Act. FOSTA/SESTA remove safe harbor for legal prostitution online. As noted in an article on *Vox* by Aja Romano, "In the immediate aftermath of SESTA's passage on March 21, 2018, numerous websites took action to censor or ban parts of their platforms in response—not because those parts of the sites actually *were* promoting ads for prostitutes, but because policing them against the outside possibility that they *might* was just too hard." For example, Craigslist removed its personals section, not just in the United States but around the world. Reddit's response was even more wide-ranging, and the company forbid the sale of firearms and explosives on its site (Reddit 2018). Although most tech companies were opposed to the bill, others, most notably ORACLE, were supportive of it, as was Hollywood, because the law would allow for additional filtering of the internet, including copyrighted material ("Senators Welcome Support" n.d.). There are now calls to reform the law and a bill to study it was introduced in the 2021–22 congressional session (Khanna 2022).

Further Reading

Harmon, Elliot. 2018. "How Congress Censored the Internet." Electronic Frontier Foundation. March 21, 2018. https://www.eff.org/deeplinks/2018/03/how-congress-censored-internet.

> This article from the Electronic Frontier Foundation provides an overview of the effects of FOSTA/SESTA. Recent updates on related topics are linked at the bottom of the web page.

Jurecic, Quinta. 2022. "The Politics of Section 230 Reform: Learning from FOSTA's Mistakes." *Brookings* (blog), March 1, 2022. https://www.brookings.edu/research/the-politics-of-section-230-reform-learning-from-fostas-mistakes/.

This article from the centrist public policy think tank Brookings Institute describes how the effects of FOSTA/SESTA intersect with possible changes to Section 230.

Mullin, Joe. 2018. "How FOSTA Could Give Hollywood the Filters It's Long Wanted." Electronic Frontier Foundation, March 16, 2018. https://www.eff.org/deeplinks/2018/03/how-fosta-will-get-hollywood-filters-theyve-long-wanted.

Mullin describes why corporate content creators support FOSTA/SESTA. This article focuses on television and movie creators and their concerns regarding intellectual property rights infringement.

York, Jillian C. 2022. "Silicon Valley's Sex Censorship Harms Everyone." *Wired*, March 18, 2022. https://www.wired.com/story/silicon-values-internet-sex-censorship/.

This article describes the immediate effects of FOSTA/SESTA on the livelihoods of sex workers and on the freedom of expression.

ARTIFICIAL INTELLIGENCE, ALGORITHMS, TRACKING, AND PRIVACY

Although artificial intelligence (AI) and tracking are not identical, they share two related issues: Who is watching what I do with information and how does that influence the information I have access to? The revelations from Edward Snowden regarding the National Security Agency's (NSA) global surveillance gave proof that our online lives are constantly monitored. Glenn Greenwald and Ewen MacAskill (2013) reported that the NSA collected search history, content of emails, file transfers, and live chats. In addition, the agency was monitoring the telephone conversations of thirty-five world leaders. The NSA's argument was that it could do this because the Foreign Intelligence Surveillance Act (FISA) process of obtaining subpoenas with attached gag orders was broken, and the agency refused to ask US FISA court judges for authorization.

Surveillance is not only carried out by the government but also by technology companies. Our every move online is tracked. It is worth the time to review one's privacy and tracking information on Google simply to see the sheer volume of information about a given person that Google collects. Facebook serves up ads based on the information its algorithm has gathered on us. It also has shadow profiles for people who do not have a profile themselves but whom the platform knows exist. Smart assistants like Alexa, Siri, and Google Assistant are always listening (Clauser 2019). However, Amazon argues that Alexa is not listening because it is waiting for the wake word (Amazon.com n.d.). Maintaining one's privacy in the wake of this ever-increasing surveillance is very difficult (Sun, Chen, and Zhang 2020).

This matters for intellectual freedom in general because algorithms and tracking work together to create "information bubbles." Technology companies thrive by providing only information that you want and not supplying information that you do not want. These "filter bubbles" mean that the communications circuit is controlled by AI and tracking. Individuals must work hard to take themselves out of an information environment that provides only certain types of information. Offline, surveillance is a constant. The presence of CCTVs and facial recognition software means that our interactions with the built world are being monitored on a regular basis.

Further Reading

"Global Surveillance Disclosures (2013-Present)." 2022. *Wikipedia, The Free Encyclopedia*. https://en.wikipedia.org/w/index.php?title=Global_surveillance_disclosures_(2013%E2%80%93present)&oldid=1081500395.

While Laura Poitras's 2014 documentary, *CitizenFour*, and Edward Snowden's own book *Permanent Record* (Metropolitan Books, 2019) provide overviews of the NSA disclosures, the Wikipedia article delivers incredible minutia on the subject along with up-to-the-minute updates and an overview of the ongoing disputes.

Hautala, Laura. n.d. "Shadow Profiles: Facebook Has Information You Didn't Hand Over." *CNET*. https://www.cnet.com/news/privacy/shadow-profiles-facebook-has-information-you-didnt-hand-over/.

Hautala describes how Facebook uses algorithms to infer data that users do not provide. As noted above, Facebook and other social media platforms can triangulate data to infer shadow profiles of people who do not use their services.

Information on the Tor Browser Project. https://www.torproject.org.

Resources from the Library Freedom Project. https://libraryfreedom.org/resources/.

MISINFORMATION, DISINFORMATION, AND MALINFORMATION

Misinformation is a mistake. Disinformation is a lie. Malinformation is false information that is shared with a "distinct intent to cause harm, and in the case of racism, to maintain the status quo" (Cooke 2021). Although it may seem straightforward, sorting out what is or is not truthful information is more of a question of interpretation rather than a question of facts. Telling people that, for instance, correlation does not equal causation when it comes to vaccines or that more white people than Black commit crimes in the United States does not necessarily change people's minds. Interpretation of facts is embedded in societal structures and language. This matters for intellectual freedom because of the effects that mitigating misinformation and disinformation might have on freedom of expression. Who decides what is misinformation and disinformation? How are they making those decisions? Who might be harmed when these decisions are made?

When former US President Donald Trump was banned from Twitter and Facebook in 2021, many cheered that decision. However, this decision also laid bare the absolute power that the few people who run Twitter and Facebook have over national and global discourse. The owners of these and other social media companies have censored many underrepresented and marginalized groups with, for example, Facebook's censorship of ostensibly female nipples on its platforms while permitting male nipples—a rule that does not make sense for people who are nonbinary.

Danielle Allen's (2015) discourse flow model is one possibility for thinking about online expression. It focuses primarily on responsibility: the bigger and more "sticky" your audience, the more responsibility you have to tell the truth and be accountable. Allen uses the ideas of flow (volume, velocity, and viscosity) to analyze which types of discourse should be subject to additional oversight measures. Cooke (2021) argues that critical cultural literacy (CCL) is a way forward. CCL combines information with media, design, political, historical, emotional, cultural, and racial literacies. This is difficult to do but is imperative when responding to the spread of misinformation and disinformation and also for supporting intellectual freedom for all.

Further Reading

Cooke, Nicole A. 2018. *Fake News and Alternative Facts: Information Literacy in a Post-Truth Era*. Chicago: American Library Association.

    This report is a primer on misinformation and disinformation. It should be read along with Cooke's 2021 article on malinformation.

———. 2021. "Tell Me Sweet Little Lies: Racism as a Form of Persistent Malinformation." *Project Information Literacy* (blog), August 11, 2021. https://projectinfolit.org/pubs/provocation-series/essays/tell-me-sweet-little-lies.html.

    This piece was written as part of the Project Information Literacy Provocation Series.

News Literacy Project. n.d. "Five Types of Misinformation." *News Literacy Project*. https://newslit.org/educators/resources/misinformation/.

    The News Literacy Project, a nonpartisan education nonprofit, offers a clear typology of misinformation and lists additional resources.

HATE SPEECH

In many ways, hate speech is an intractable problem as there is no doubt that it both leads to mental harm and can result in physical violence. The question is what should be done in response. Outlawing hate speech is a blunt instrument. This can be seen in the current upheavals across the United States regarding critical race theory (CRT). These controversies are, of course, not about the theory developed by Derrick Bell and others but about an idea of history and how it should be taught.

The organization No Left Turn argues that:

> [CRT] is a neo-Marxist-type ideology that replaces the Marxist idea of class conflict between capitalists and workers with the idea of racial conflict.... This racist, discriminatory, divisive, and self-flagellating ideology is metastasizing throughout America's corporations, medical facilities, the military, educational institutions, and most disturbingly, in our K-12 school. (https://www.noleftturn.us/crt-code-words/#)

No Left Turn's website includes a list of "code words" that have been recoded as "hate speech." There is an argument that there should be some repository for monitoring hate speech. For example, the Southern Poverty Law Center maintains a map of hate groups (https://www.splcenter.org/hate-map). However, as with so many of these issues, these groups are only considered hate groups by some. For example, the Family Research Council is listed as a hate group to the consternation of many conservatives (Smith 2019).

We live in a colonialist, racist, sexist, heterosexist, ableist, white supremacist world, and language is slippery. In addition, deciding what is or is not hate speech often puts power into the hands of the already powerful. It is not those who will be harmed by hate speech that will make these decisions, but Mark Zuckerberg, Sundar Pichai, and the United States Supreme Court.

Further Reading

Bennett, Jessica. 2020. "What If Instead of Calling People Out, We Called Them In?" *The New York Times*, November 19, 2020. https://www.nytimes.com/2020/11/19/style/loretta-ross-smith-college-cancel-culture.html.

    This profile of Loretta J. Ross (https://lorettajross.com) describes her philosophy of "calling in" in response to hateful language and behavior. Ross has worked extensively with members of white supremacist groups.

Delgado, Richard, and Jean Stefancic. 2018. *Must We Defend Nazis?: Why the First Amendment Should Not Protect Hate Speech and White Supremacy*. New York: New York University Press.

This follow-up to *Words That Wound* (Westview Press 1993), written for a general audience, offers an argument for outlawing hate speech. Delgado and Stefancic claim that the current legal framework for the First Amendment law is too broad and leads to harm.

Strossen, Nadine. 2018. "Counterspeech in Response to Changing Notions of Free Speech." *Human Rights Magazine*, October 20, 2018. https://www.americanbar.org/groups/crsj/publications/human_rights_magazine_home/the-ongoing-challenge-to-define-free-speech/counterspeech-in-response-to-free-speech/.

Strossen, a former president of the ACLU, argues for counterspeech as a response to hate speech. This argument is further developed in her monograph *HATE: Why We Should Resist It with Free Speech, Not Censorship* (Oxford 2020).

MATERIALS CHALLENGES

Challenges to materials in public institutions, especially books, ebb and flow depending on societal changes. In the latter months of 2021, the dam burst on book challenges in the United States. According to Deborah Caldwell-Stone, director of ALA's Office for Intellectual Freedom, the number of reported book bans tripled in late 2021:

> We received 377 reports for the entire year. Between Sept. 1 and Nov. 30, 2021, we received 330. And the phenomenon continues at a rate I've not seen in my 20 years with ALA. We're seeing organized campaigns from groups styled as parent rights organizations. (Caldwell-Stone, as quoted in Varine 2022)

These materials challenges have generally been against what might be called diverse books or books that center on the lives of "LGBTQIA, Native, people of color, gender diversity, people with disabilities, and ethnic, cultural, and religious minorities." (Note that use of the word "disability" "includes but is not limited to physical, sensory, cognitive, intellectual, or developmental disabilities, chronic conditions, and mental illnesses [this may also include addiction]. Furthermore, we subscribe to a social model of disability, which presents disability as created by barriers in the social environment, due to lack of equal access, stereotyping, and other forms of marginalization" [We Need Diverse Books n.d.]).

Although books such as *All Boys Aren't Blue* by George M. Johnson, *Gender Queer* by Maia Kobabe, *Out of Darkness* by Ashley Hope Pérez, and others were challenged, the removal of *Maus* by Art Spiegelman galvanized many more people to the anti-censorship cause. Many of these challenges center on graphic narratives, both fiction and nonfiction. This newish genre is one that requires new forms of interpretation, and often parents, who might be comfortable with certain texts, are uncomfortable when, for example, sexual situations are shown in images.

These challenges are also closely aligned with the anti-critical race theory crusades described above, and there is no sign that they will stop soon. As the world moves through the end of the COVID-19 pandemic, and we contend with other divisive crises such as war, unrest, and climate change, there will continue to be challenges to materials. In the United States, for example, we have not yet grappled with the insurrection of January 6, 2021. That historical event has not yet been included in textbooks or incorporated into mainstream curricula. It is unknown what the response to its inclusion will be. Librarians and other information professionals must remain vigilant in the face of these challenges.

Further Reading

EveryLibrary, "Book Censorship Database." https://www.everylibraryinstitute.org/book_censorship_database_magnusson.

Harris, Elizabeth A., and Alexandra Alter. 2022. "Book Ban Efforts Spread Across the U.S." *The New York Times*, January 30, 2022. https://www.nytimes.com/2022/01/30/books/book-ban-us-schools.html.

    Harris and Alter's long-form article gives an overview of the political landscape for book banning. It provides an excellent overview for a general audience.

Higgins-Dailey, Jacqui. 2022. "The Stakeholders of Status Quo." *Intellectual Freedom Blog*, March 10, 2022. https://www.oif.ala.org/oif/the-stakeholders-of-status-quo/.

    This post provides information on several organizations that work to remove materials in public institutions. The Intellectual Freedom Blog provides intellectual freedom news and analysis every week.

National Coalition Against Censorship. "Youth Censorship Database." https://ncac.org/youth-censorship-database.

    The National Coalition Against Censorship and EveryLibrary—working with Dr. Tasslyn Magnusson—track book challenges in real time in these databases.

ANTI-INTELLECTUAL FREEDOM LAWS

Along with the materials challenges, anti-critical race theory, and concerns over sexual orientation and gender identity, there are also a growing number of anti-intellectual freedom laws being passed across the United States. Some legislation directly targets curricula such as those that would make it illegal to teach the 1619 Project in school curriculum (Rodriguez 2021). At the time of this writing, Florida has passed a so-called "Don't Say Gay" law that limits freedom of expression in K-12 schools (Goldstein 2022). This law makes it illegal to include classroom instruction on sexual orientation or gender identity in kindergarten through third grade. The language of the bill also implies that there should not be any classroom discussion of these two topics in any grade. Parents can sue schools for violating this law. This legislation places knowledge circulation in the hands of an unknown judiciary. Despite its stated goals of reinforcing community values, it takes education out of the hands of parents or teachers.

    In addition, states have passed laws that would make it a criminal offense for libraries or schools to provide information that someone deems inappropriate. As of early 2022, similar bills are under consideration in Indiana and Iowa. The Iowa bill focuses on obscenity and would allow for lawsuits that could result in $10,000 minimum awards to parents or guardians. The Indiana bill, it should be noted, is related to the code titled "Dissemination of Matter or Conducting Performance Harmful to Minors." Although intended to focus on pornography, as David Sye (2022) notes, public testimony focused on *How to Be an Antiracist* by Ibram X. Kendi, *It's Perfectly Normal* by Robie Harris, and *George* by Alex Gino, all of which were called obscene.

    Along with these laws, several libraries have been subject to so-called "First Amendment Audits," where members of the public record video inside library buildings to capture a record of "constitutional violations" (Balzar 2022). Individual teachers and librarians are also being targeted. For example, an elementary school vice principal was fired for simply reading aloud *I Need a New Butt* by Dawn McMillan, a book intended for ages six to ten (Cramer and Paz 2022).

    These bills, laws, and audits are disturbing, and it is likely that they will have a chilling effect on librarians' and teachers' professional practice. They are efforts to criminalize intellectual freedom and entrench censorship in public institutions. More than that, they put strictures on service positions. It is difficult to know how we will be able to encourage people to choose to be teachers and school librarians.

Further Reading

Caldwell-Stone, Deborah. 2019. "Auditing the First Amendment at Your Public Library." *Intellectual Freedom Blog,* October 2, 2019. https://www.oif.ala.org/oif/auditing-the-first-amendment-at-your-public-library/.

This article is from the Intellectual Freedom Blog published by ALA's Office for Intellectual Freedom. First Amendment audits are a harassment tactic used by activists to intimidate library workers. This blog post provides guidance and resources for libraries and other institutions that have been targeted.

Lechtenberg, Kate. 2020. "Missouri, Florida, and the Criminalization of Libraries." *Intellectual Freedom Blog,* February 24, 2020. https://www.oif.ala.org/oif/missouri-florida-and-the-criminalization-of-libraries/.

In this article, Lechtenberg describes proposed laws in Missouri and Florida and their potential intellectual freedom consequences. She also provides tips for what people can do to counter these proposed measures.

EveryLibrary. 2021. "Iowa: Criminalizing Books and Arresting Teachers and Librarians." *EveryLibrary Action,* December 6, 2021. https://action.everylibrary.org/iowa_is_criminalizing_books_and_threatening_teachers_and_librarians_with_incarceration.

This call to action from the EveryLibrary political action committee is an example of political action on behalf of libraries. Intellectual freedom supporters should be aware of international, national, state, and local efforts to advocate for intellectual freedom and related rights.

CHALLENGES AHEAD (PUN INTENDED)

The human right to intellectual freedom is constantly critiqued and attacked. The desire to curb the circulation of information is a distinctly human one. Information can change how someone understands the world—and not always for the better. Intellectual freedom and censorship are wrapped up in issues of knowledge, symbolism, power, and ideas about how one should live in the world. The transmission of knowledge from one generation to the next is vitally important to our understanding of what it means to be human. This is why the impulse to censor is so strong—how can we guarantee that the next generation will have the right values no matter how we might define those? Certainly, there are no guarantees, but censorship hedges the bet that at least certain types of knowledge might not reach a particular population.

Intellectual freedom is the right of every individual to hold and express opinions and seek, access, receive, and impart information ideas without restriction. This definition is, of course, almost impossible to put into practice. We restrict ideas for a host of reasons. Perhaps some information is deemed by a government to be too dangerous for general circulation. Perhaps certain information is not appropriate at a child's stage of development. Perhaps some information should remain private. These all can be legitimate reasons for engaging in censorship practices. What matters is the analysis of why someone is engaging in these practices. Are they making decisions for other people that people should only make for themselves? Is the government actually hiding corruption? Does a parent truly want their child to be ignorant of certain truths about human behavior and the world? Does withholding certain private information lead to bias and discrimination?

Although these questions are difficult to answer, they are vital as we move forward. Our responses to the major societal changes of our age will rest on our understanding of the issues. If petroleum companies, the wealthiest companies in the history of the world, decide that all of their knowledge is a trade secret, it will be increasingly difficult to respond to climate change. Responses to the COVID-19 pandemic meant that many of us had to be willing to give up our right to medical privacy to ensure that others did not get sick and die. And we still have not found adequate ways to respond to the deluge of information that is available on the computing devices that we carry on our persons every day.

The easiest answer is simply to shut it all down. If some type of information will be harmful in some way, just get rid of it. However, this response always leads to a power imbalance and it is the height of paternalism. Someone has made a decision for you and in some cases you will not even know that the decision has been made. This is most easily seen in the case of personal data privacy where, as Daniel Solove (2007) argues, "the issue is not about whether or not the information gathered is something people want to hide but rather the power and the structure of government" (767).

This is also true in other matters related to intellectual freedom. For example, when a book is removed from a library because someone disagrees with its contents, that person or system has placed themselves in the powerful position of deciding what is best for every individual in the community. If there was not a formal process for removing the book, the community might not even know that it is gone. Selection, on the other hand, compels the person in power to look for a reason to provide the information (Asheim 1953).

When it comes to issues of hate speech and similar harmful content, the impulse toward paternalism and censorship is even stronger. However, even though these drives come from a place of caring, they are still putting someone or a system in a position of power over others. Censorship of hate speech, misinformation, and disinformation assumes that it is possible to predict what the outcome of encountering that information will be. As noted above, this does not always mean that censorship of these types of speech is wrong in every case, but such action should only be taken after a thorough analysis of the power dynamics involved, an awareness that interpretation matters, and that one person's understanding as well as the effect of these materials will be different from another person's.

Books like this one rarely end with a call to action, but it is necessary here given the current threats to intellectual freedom both in the United States and around the world. As South African librarian Ellen Tise, IFLA president from 2009-2011 and chair of IFLA's Advisory Committee on Freedom of Access to Information and Freedom of Expression (2019-2021), stated in an interview: "libraries should form strategic partnerships with Governments, Development Agencies, Human rights organisations to ensure social inclusion, promote education, encourage freedom of opinion and expression, affirm intellectual freedom and the protection of human rights" (IFLA 2021). It is imperative that librarians and other information professionals stand up for the right to information access in the public sphere. This will require being both personally and institutionally prepared to respond to censorship as well as organizing and advocating for intellectual freedom locally, nationally, and globally.

REFERENCES

Allen, Danielle S. 2015. "Reconceiving Public Spheres: The Flow Dynamics Model." In *From Voice to Influence: Understanding Citizenship in a Digital Age*, edited by Danielle S. Allen and Jennifer S. Light, 178–207. Chicago; London: The University of Chicago Press.

Amazon.com. n.d. "Is Alexa Always Listening?" https://www.amazon.com/is-alexa-always-listening/b?ie=UTF8&node=21137869011.

Asheim, L. 1953. "Not Censorship but Selection." *Wilson Library Bulletin* 28 (1): 63–67.

Balzar, Cass. 2022. "Uptick in First Amendment Audits." *American Libraries*, January 23, 2022. https://americanlibrariesmagazine.org/?p=127408.

Chandel, Sonali, Zang Jingji, Yu Yunnan, Sun Jingyao, and Zhang Zhipeng. 2019. "The Golden Shield Project of China: A Decade Later—An In-Depth Study of the Great Firewall." In *2019 International Conference on Cyber-Enabled Distributed Computing and Knowledge Discovery (CyberC)*, 111–19. https://doi.org/10.1109/CyberC.2019.00027.

Clauser, Grant. 2019. "Amazon's Alexa Never Stops Listening to You. Should You Worry?" *Wirecutter: Reviews for the Real World*, August 8, 2019. https://www.nytimes.com/wirecutter/blog/amazons-alexa-never-stops-listening-to-you/.

Cooke, Nicole A. 2021. "Tell Me Sweet Little Lies: Racism as a Form of Persistent Malinformation." PIL Provocation Series, *Project Information Literacy* (blog), August 11, 2021. https://projectinfolit.org/pubs/provocation-series/essays/tell-me-sweet-little-lies.html.

Cramer, Maria, and Isabella Grullón Paz. 2022. "An Educator Read 'I Need a New Butt!' to Children. Then He Was Fired." *The New York Times*, March 11, 2022. https://www.nytimes.com/2022/03/11/us/toby-price-mississippi.html.

Freedom House. 2021. "In Iran, Authorities Defend an Illegitimate Election by Suppressing Online Dissent." June 14, 2021. https://freedomhouse.org/article/iran-authorities-defend-illegitimate-election-suppressing-online-dissent.

Goldstein, Dana. 2022. "Opponents Call It the 'Don't Say Gay' Bill. Here's What It Says." *The New York Times*, March 18, 2022. https://www.nytimes.com/2022/03/18/us/dont-say-gay-bill-florida.html.

Greenwald, Glenn, and Ewen MacAskill. 2013. "NSA Prism Program Taps in to User Data of Apple, Google and Others." *The Guardian*, June 7, 2013. www.theguardian.com/world/2013/jun/06/us-tech-giants-nsa-data.

IFLA. 2021. "Libraries for Human Rights: An Interview with Ellen Tise, Chair, IFLA Advisory Committee on Freedom of Access to Information and Freedom of Expression." December 1, 2021. https://www.ifla.org/news/libraries-for-human-rights-an-interview-with-ellen-tise-chair-ifla-advisory-committee-on-freedom-of-access-to-information-and-freedom-of-expression/.

Khanna, Ro. 2022. "H.R.6928—117th Congress (2021-2022): SAFE SEX Workers Study Act." Legislation. 2021/2022. March 3, 2022. https://www.congress.gov/bill/117th-congress/house-bill/6928.

Reddit. 2018. "New Addition to Site-Wide Rules Regarding the Use of Reddit to Conduct Transactions." *R/Announcements*. www.reddit.com/r/announcements/comments/863xcj/new_addition_to_sitewide_rules_regarding_the_use/.

Rodriguez, Barbara. 2021. "Slavery History: States Threaten Funds for Schools Teaching 1619 Project." *USA Today*, February 10, 2021. https://www.usatoday.com/story/news/education/2021/02/10/slavery-and-history-states-threaten-funding-schools-teach-1619-project/4454195001/.

Romano, Aja. 2018. "A New Law Intended to Curb Sex Trafficking Threatens the Future of the Internet as We Know It." *Vox*, July 2, 2018. https://www.vox.com/culture/2018/4/13/17172762/fosta-sesta-backpage-230-internet-freedom.

"Senators Welcome Support from Tech Giant Oracle for the Stop Enabling Sex Traffickers Act." Newsroom, Senator Rob Portman, September 6, 2017. https://www.portman.senate.gov/newsroom/press-releases/senators-welcome-support-tech-giant-oracle-stop-enabling-sex-traffickers.

Smith, Jessica Prol. 2019. "The Southern Poverty Law Center Is a Hate-Based Scam That Nearly Caused Me to Be Murdered." *USA Today*, August 17, 2019. https://www.usatoday.com/story/opinion/2019/08/17/southern-poverty-law-center-hate-groups-scam-column/2022301001/.

Solove, Daniel J. 2007. "'I've Got Nothing to Hide' and Other Misunderstandings of Privacy." SSRN Scholarly Paper ID 998565. Rochester, NY: Social Science Research Network. http://papers.ssrn.com/abstract=998565.

Sun, Ke, Chen Chen, and Xinyu Zhang. 2020. "'Alexa, Stop Spying on Me!': Speech Privacy Protection against Voice Assistants." In *Proceedings of the 18th Conference on Embedded Networked Sensor Systems*, 298–311. New York: Association for Computing Machinery. https://doi.org/10.1145/3384419.3430727.

Sye, David. 2022. "Beyond Book Banning: Efforts to Criminally Charge Librarians." *Intellectual Freedom Blog,* March 8, 2022. https://www.oif.ala.org/oif/beyond-book-banning-efforts-to-criminally-charge-librarians/.

Varine, Patrick. 2022. "Book Challenges Are Becoming More Frequent, Driven in Part by Social Media." TribLIVE.Com. *Tribune Review*, March 14, 2022. https://triblive.com/local/westmoreland/book-challenges-are-becoming-more-frequent-driven-in-part-by-social-media/.

We Need Diverse Books. n.d. "Our Definition of Diversity." https://diversebooks.org/about-wndb/.

INDEX

#
1619 Project, 116
1976 Copyright Act, 86-88
1998 Copyright Term Extension Act, 92-93

A
access
    censorship and, 62-66
    as facet of intellectual freedom, 9-10, 53-55
    policies for, 56-61
    types of, 55-56, 61-62
Against Free Speech (Leaker), 41
Albanese, Andrew, 94
Alfino, Mark, 13
algorithms, 104, 112-113
Allen, Danielle S., 113
Alter, Alexandra, 116
Amazon, 71, 88, 91-92, 112
American Civil Liberties Union (ACLU), 5
American Libraries, 35
American Library Association (ALA)
    Code of Ethics, 10-11, 28, 53-54, 69, 84, 104-105
    court cases tracked by, 26
    Field Report: Banned and Challenged Books, 19, 65
    Freedom to Read Statement, 10, 58, 100-101, 103
    Freedom to View Statement, 10, 58, 103
    Intellectual Freedom Committee, 99, 102
    Library Bill of Rights, 10, 58-59, 78, 79, 97-99, 103
    motto of, 28
    Office for Intellectual Freedom, 1, 14, 30, 46, 65, 102, 117
    societal change and, 101-102
anti-intellectual freedom laws, 116-117
"Apathy, Convenience or Irrelevance?" (Keen), 81
Areopagitica (Milton), 19, 31
art, visual, 40, 63, 85, 93
Article 19 (of Universal Declaration of Human Rights), 2, 11, 25, 36-37, 53, 84, 87
ARTICLE 19 (organization), 2, 26, 37, 43-44
artificial intelligence (AI), 104, 112
Asheim, Lester, 64, 100
Association for Information Science and Technology (ASIS&T), 65, 84, 97
Atkins, Robert, 13
authors, rights of, 85-88, 92, 93
autonomy, 1, 2-3, 54-55, 77

B
Bald, Margaret, 19, 66
Banned Books Week, 103
Barbakoff, Audrey, 3, 54-55
Beisel, Nicola, 30
Belarde-Lewis, Miranda H., 65
Benn, Piers, 2, 13
Bennett, Jessica, 114
Bennett, Steven C., 74
Berger, Peter L., 9
Berne Convention, 86
Berninghausen, David, 102
Beyond Banned Books (Pekoll), 107
bias, as passive censorship, 64
Biden, Joe, 43
Big-P policy, 57, 66
BIPOC, as term, 39
Black Lives Matter (BLM), 7, 42, 45, 104
Black Scholar, 71-72, 81
Board of Education, Island Trees Union Free School District v. Pico, 27
Bocher, Joseph, 38
Book Banning in 21st-Century America (Knox), 2
Book Riot, 46, 69
books
    challenges to, ix, 8, 19, 42, 46, 62-64, 107, 115-116
    selection of, 59, 100-101
    that were considered trashy, 98
Books on Trial (Wiegand), 31
Boyer, Paul, 30
Bradbury, Ray, 66
Braman, Sandra, 57, 66
Brandenburg v. Ohio, 27
Britz, Johannes J., 10, 54
Brownson, Ross C., 57
Brugger, Winfried, 43
Budd, John, 4

Burgess, G. Scott, 110
Burgess, John, 3, 106
Burke, Peter, 8
Burke, Susan K., 10-11
Burn This Book (Morrison), 66
Byrne, Alex, 29, 30

C

Cage, John, 40
Caldwell-Stone, Deborah, 115, 117
California Consumer Privacy Act (CCPA), 77
calling in, 40-41, 114
cancel culture, 40-41
The Case against Free Speech (Moskowitz), 43
Censoring Culture (Atkins et al.), 13
censorship
    definitions of, 4-6
    of difficult knowledge, 9, 110
    further reading on, 30-31, 65-66, 110-112, 116
    history of, 18-20
    information access and, 53-55, 62-66
    internet filtering as, 11, 77-78, 109-110
    justifications for, 64
    practices of, 5-6, 62-64
    selection and, 100-101
challenges to materials, ix, 8, 19, 42, 46, 62-64, 107, 115-116
Champaign Public Library, 59
Chancellor, R. L., 106
Change of State (Braman), 66
Chaplinsky v. New Hampshire, 38-39
Chen, Alan K., 38
Chicago Public Library Board, 28, 98
child pornography, 27, 37-38
children, rights of, 27, 77-78
Children's Online Privacy Protection Act (COPPA), 77
Chiu, Anastasia, 24
Chmara, Theresa, 27
Chriqui, Jamie F., 57
Cleveland, Sarah H., 43
Coates, Ta-Nehisi, 18
Code of Ethics, ALA, 10-11, 28, 53-54, 69, 84, 104-105
communication, as linchpin right, 3, 26
Communications Decency Act, 110-111
communities, interpretive, 37, 39-41, 42, 45
"Concepts of Intellectual Freedom and Copyright" (Moore), 95
confidentiality, 70, 79. See also privacy
Connolly, Matthew, 79
consequentialism, 22
conservative pundits, 41
contextual integrity, 72-74
Contrapoints (YouTube channel), 40
convenience, privacy and, 70-71
Cooke, Louise, 6
Cooke, Nicole A., 106, 113-114
cookie banners, 76
copyright, 83-95
Copyright Act (1976), 86-88
Copyright Law for Librarians and Educators (Crews), 94
"Counterspeech in Response to Changing Notions of Free Speech" (Strossen), 115
court cases, 26-28, 38-39, 89-90
COVID-19, 73, 106, 118
Creating Policies for Results (Nelson and Garcia), 57-58, 66
Creative Commons, 93, 94
"The Creed of a Librarian" (Foskett), 24
Crews, Kenneth, 87, 90-91, 94
critical cultural literacy (CCL), 113
critical librarianship, 6-7, 105
critical race theory (CRT), 7, 42, 45, 114
Critlib.org, 6
Ctrl + Z (Jones), 80

D

Dag Hammarskjöld Library, 25, 60
Dahlen, S. P., 106
Dare to Speak (Nossel), 48
Darnton, Robert, 37, 54
Data Scientist Association, 79
Dawson, Juno, 63
De Tocqueville, Alexis, 21
decision heuristics, 73-74
Delgado, Richard, 48, 115
Dellinger, Hannah, 110
Democracy in America (De Tocqueville), 21
democratic ideals, 1, 4, 21, 100
depository libraries, 62
Dick, Kirby, 66
difficult knowledge, 9, 110
digital divide, 55-56
Digital Millennium Copyright Act, 91-92
disinformation and misinformation, 56, 99, 113-114
The Dismissal of Miss Ruth Brown (Robbins), 31
Disney, as copyright holder, 83, 92
diverse books, challenges to, 115
dog whistling, 35-36
"Don't Say Gay" law, 116
Douglas, William O., 23

Douglass, Frederick, 45
Doyle, Arthur Conan, 92-93
Dresang, Eliza, 2, 10
droit moral, 85, 86, 93

E

Electronic Frontier Foundation, 111, 112
Ellis, Danika, 46
embeddedness of language, 39-40, 42-45
Emerson, Thomas Irwin, 37-38
Encyclopedia of Censorship (Green and Karolides), 18, 30
Enola Holmes series, 92-93
ethics, code of, 10-11, 28, 53-54, 69, 84, 104-105
Ettarh, Fobazi M., 24
Eubanks, Virgina, 55
European Union, laws in, 42-44, 75-77
EveryLibrary, 116, 117
expression, freedom of, 13, 20-21, 26-28, 35-48, 83-84, 110, 116

F

Facebook, 71, 110, 111, 112, 113
Facts on File, 18, 19, 66
Fahrenheit 451 (Bradbury), 66
fair use, 89, 90-91
Farkas, Meredith, 35
Ferretti, Jennifer A., 24, 89-90
Field Report: Banned and Challenged Books (ALA), 19, 65
Fight Online Sex Trafficking Act (FOSTA), 111-112
fighting words, 27, 37-39
filtering and firewalls, 11, 77-78, 109-110
Finan, Chris, 45, 47
First Amendment law, 11, 26-28, 38-39, 115, 117
first sale, right of, 89-90
Fish, Stanley, 37, 40, 43
Fiske Report, 100
Florida, "Don't Say Gay" law in, 116
flourishing, 2-3
Forbidden Books in American Public Libraries (Geller), 30, 98
forgotten, right to be, 74-75, 80
Foskett, D. J., 24
Foundations of Information Ethics (Knox), 53
Foundations of Information Policy (Jaeger and Taylor), 66
free speech, 1, 17, 37, 38, 41-42, 45-46, 47-48
Free Speech (Mchangama), 48
Freedman, Jenna, 104, 105
freedom of expression, 13, 20-21, 26-28, 35-48, 83-84, 110, 116

Freedom of Information Act, 61-62
Freedom to Read Foundation, ix, 11
Freedom to Read Statement, 10, 58, 100-101, 103
Freedom to View Statement, 10, 58, 103
Fuchs, Christian, 71
Fundamentals of Information Studies (Lester and Koehler), 10

G

Gaffney, Loretta, ix, 66
Gajda, Amy, 80
Garcia, June, 57-58, 60-61, 66
Garnar, Martin, 14, 30
Gebru, Timnit, 104
Geertz, Clifford, 39
Geller, Evelyn, 28, 30, 97, 98
General Data Protection Regulation (GDPR), 74-77
Germany, laws in, 43, 44
Gibson, A. N., 106
"Global Surveillance Disclosures" (Wikipedia), 80, 113
Google
    algorithms of, 104, 112
    right to be forgotten and, 74-75
Google Books, 17, 88
Google's Ngram, 17
Gorman, Michael, 103
Green, Jonathon, 30
Greenwald, Glenn, 80, 112
Greshake, Bastian, 94
Griswold v. Connecticut, 27
guidelines, development of, 58

H

harm principle, 22-23
Harmon, Elliot, 111
Harris, Elizabeth A., 116
Harris, Robie, 8, 116
HATE (Strossen), 48
hate speech, 25, 35-36, 42-45, 48, 114-115, 118
Hautala, Laura, 113
Health Insurance Portability and Accountability Act (HIPPA), 77
Heller, Michael A., 94
Higgins-Dailey, Jacqui, 116
A History of ALA Policy on Intellectual Freedom (Garnar and Magi), 30
Holmes, Oliver Wendell, 23, 27
Houghton, Sarah, 110
How Free Speech Saved Democracy (Finan), 47
human rights
    intellectual freedom and, 2-4, 24-26, 29

UN Universal Declaration of, 2, 24-26, 28-29, 36, 37, 53, 84, 87

I

Imperiled Innocents (Beisel), 30
In the Night Kitchen (Sendak), 63
"The Inconsistent Work of Web Filters" (Peterson et al.), 110
Index on Censorship, 26
individual autonomy, 1, 2-3, 54-55, 77
information access
    censorship and, 62-66
    as facet of intellectual freedom, 9-10, 53-55
    policies for, 56-61
    types of, 55-56, 61-62
information collection, 72
information communication technology (ICT), 54
information dissemination, 72
information institutions, privacy in, 78-80
information invasion, 72
information processing, 72
information professions, 97-107
Instagram, 36
intellectual freedom
    areas of, 9-11
    copyright and, 83-95
    as a core value, 1, 28-29, 53, 97-107
    current and future issues in, 109-118
    definitions of, 1-2, 117
    as a democratic ideal, 1, 4, 21, 100
    freedom of expression and, 13, 20-21, 26-28, 35-48, 83-84, 110, 116
    history of, 17-29
    human rights and, 2-4, 24-26, 29
    information access as facet of, 9-10, 53-55
    information professions and, 97-107
    privacy and, 9, 11, 27, 69-81
    See also censorship
Intellectual Freedom and the Culture Wars (Benn), 13
Intellectual Freedom Committee (IFC), 99, 102
Intellectual Freedom Manual (Magi and Garnar), 1, 12, 14, 26, 61, 79
Intellectual Freedom Stories from a Shifting Landscape (Nye), 107
intellectual property, 54, 83-86, 95
International Federation of Library Associations and Institutions (IFLA), 28-29, 30, 53-54, 118
international law, 37, 42-44, 75-77, 83, 86
internet filtering, 11, 77-78, 109-110
The Internet's Own Boy (Knappenberger), 95

interpretive communities, 37, 39-41, 42, 45
Is There a Text in This Class? (Fish), 40
Islands of Privacy (Nippert-Eng), 71
"It Needs to Be Accessible by All" (Dellinger), 110
It's Perfectly Normal (Harris), 8, 116
"I've Got Nothing to Hide" (Solove), 71

J

Jacobs, Samuel, 86
Jaeger, Paul T., 66
Jansen, Sue Curry, 2, 4, 5
Jones, Meg Leta, 80
Josey, E. J., 102
Joyce, Stephen, 104
Jurecic, Quinta, 112

K

Karolides, Nicholas J., 18-19, 30
Keen, Caroline, 81
Kennedy, Randall, 42, 44-45, 48
Khalid, Amna, 47
Kirtsaeng v. John Wiley & Sons, Inc., 89
Knappenberger, Brian, 95
knowledge
    difficult, 9, 110
    sociology of, 7-9
Knowledge Justice (Leung and Lopez-McKnight), 7, 13
Knox, Emily J. M., 2, 53, 110
Koehler, Wallace C., 10
Koltutsky, Laura, 13
Kostelecky, Sarah R., 65
Krug, Judith, 102, 103

L

Labaree, Robert V., 46-47
Ladenson, Elisabeth, 30
language, embeddedness of, 39-40, 42-45
LaRue, James, 107
Latham, Joyce M., 28, 98
Latinx, as term, 39
law, international, 37, 42-44, 75-77, 83, 86
law, United States, 26-28, 37-39, 43, 61-62, 76-77, 83-95, 110-112, 116-117
Leaker, Anthony, 41
Lechtenberg, Kate, 117
legal cases, 26-28, 38-39, 89-90
Lester, June, 10
"Let's Go Brandon" chant, 43
Leung, Sofia, 7, 13
LGBTQ+ materials, 46, 110, 115

librarianship
　critical movement of, 6–7, 105
　intellectual freedom as core value in, 1, 28–29, 53, 97–107
　neutrality of, 24, 98, 101–102, 103–104
　professional values of, 10, 103–104
Library Bill of Rights, 10, 58–59, 78, 79, 97–99, 103
Library Freedom Project, 79–80, 113
Library Journal, 102
The Library Juice Press Handbook of Intellectual Freedom (Alfino and Koltutsky), 13
linchpin rights, 3, 26
Liptak, Adam, 41
Little-p policy, 57, 66
"Looking into Pandora's Box" (Greshake), 94
López-McKnight, Jorge, 7, 13
Lor, Peter, 10, 54
Lowenthal, Marjorie Fiske, 100
Luckmann, Thomas, 9

M

MacAskill, Ewen, 80, 112
MacKinnon, Catharine A., 41
"Macmillan Abandons Library E-Book Embargo" (Albanese), 94
Magi, Trina J., 14, 30
malinformation, 113–114
Mapping Information Access team, 107, 109, 110
marketplace of ideas, 1, 22–24, 26
Martin v. City of Struthers, 27
Martucci, Maria Clara, 110
materials challenges, ix, 8, 19, 42, 46, 62–64, 107, 115–116
Mathiesen, Kay, 3, 26, 55
Matsuda, Mari J., 43, 48
Matthews, Miriam, 105–106
Maus (Spiegelman), 63, 115
Mchangama, Jacob, 45, 46, 48
McMenemy, David, 24
Meiss, Mark, 11
Menczer, Filippo, 11
Merriam Webster, 5, 36
Meta, 20, 110, 111
Mickey Mouse, 83, 92
Mill, John Stuart, 12, 17, 21–24, 30
Miller Test, 27, 38
Miller v. California, 27, 38
Milton, John, 19, 31
Mine! (Heller and Salzman), 94
minors, rights for, 27, 77–78
Mintcheva, Svetlana, 13

misinformation and disinformation, 56, 99, 113–114
mission statements, 58
Moms for Liberty, 42
Monahan, Torin, 70
Moore, Adam D., 95
moral rights (droit moral), 85, 86, 87, 89, 93
morals vs. values, 10, 103–104
Morrison, Toni, 66
Morsink, Johannes, 25
Moskowitz, P. E., 43
Mullin, Joe, 112
Must We Defend Nazis? (Delgado and Stefanic), 115

N

National Coalition Against Censorship (NCAC), 13, 47, 103, 116
Nelson, Sandra, 57–58, 60–61, 66
neutrality, 24, 98, 101–102, 103–104
The New Inquisition (LaRue), 107
New York Times, 41, 114, 116
New Zealand, 44
Newman, Robin, 87–88
Newmyer, Jody, 93
News Literacy Project, 114
Nippert-Eng, Christena, 71
Nissenbaum, Helen, 72–74, 80, 81
No Left Turn, 114
Noble, Safiya Umoja, 75
Nossel, Suzanne, 46, 48
"Not Censorship but Selection" (Asheim), 100
Nothing to Hide (Solove), 81
"NSA Prism Program" (Greenwald and MacAskill), 80
Nye, Valerie, 107

O

obscenity laws, 20, 27, 38–39, 116
Ocasio-Cortez, Alexandria, 40
offensive materials, 38–39
Office for Intellectual Freedom (OIF), 1, 14, 30, 46, 65, 102, 117
Oltmann, Shannon, 1, 6, 107, 110
On Liberty (Mill), 17, 21–22, 30
"Online Censorship and Digital Surveillance" (Stoycheff et al.), 110
Open Access (Suber), 95
open access movement, 93, 95
open records laws, 61–62
orphan works, 92

Our Enduring Values Revisited (Gorman), 103
Overman, Tom, 42

P
Parker, Richard A., 23-24
Parsons, Talcott, 98
patents, 84
Patin, B., 106
Pekoll, Kristin, 62, 93, 107
permission slips, 63
personally identifiable information (PII), 70
Peterson, Chris, 110
Petley, Julian, 19
philosophy, 9-10
policies, characteristics of, 56-58
policy development
    as area of intellectual freedom, 9-11
    for information access, 58-61
policy statements, 58
Politico, 44
The Politics of Promoting Freedom of Information and Expression (Byrne), 30
Popowich, Sam, 23
Practicing Intellectual Freedom in Libraries (Oltmann), 107
Price, Richard S., 78
privacy, 9, 11, 27, 69-81, 112
"Privacy, Press, and the Right to Be Forgotten in the United States" (Gajda), 80
Privacy in Context (Nissenbaum), 72-74, 81
procedures, development of, 60-61
professional values, 103-105
propaganda, 99
public domain, 83, 88, 92
Purity in Print (Boyer), 30

R
Raber, Douglas, 101
racism, 7, 42, 44-45, 46, 114
Ratcliffe, Caitlin, 17, 20-21
Rauschenberg, Robert, 40
RAV v. St. Paul, 39
Rawls, John, 10, 23, 54, 55
"Reconciling Social Responsibility and Neutrality" (Burgess), 106
redaction, 6, 62-63
Reddit, 111
regulations, 59-60, 75-77
relocation, 6, 63
removal, 6, 63
restriction, 6, 63

rights
    to be forgotten, 74-75, 80
    of first sale, 89-90
    to intellectual property (see copyright)
    linchpin vs. primary, 3, 26
    of minors, 27, 77-78
    See also human rights
rights theory, 26
Robbins, Louise S., 30, 31, 99-100, 101
Robinson, Kerry H., 9
romance novels, 69
Romano, Aja, 111
Rosen, Jeffrey, 74
Ross, Loretta, 40-41, 114
Ryan, Alan, 21

S
safe harbor laws, 110-111
Salzman, James, 94
Samek, Toni, 6, 30, 101, 102
Saunders, Laura, 103-104
Say It Loud! (Kennedy), 44-45, 48
Schenk v. United States, 26-27
Schrader, A. M., 107
Scimeca, Ross, 46-47
Scott, Dani, 103-104
Section 230 statue, 110-111
security, convenience and, 70-71
Seiter, Alessandra, 29
selection policies, 59, 100-101
self-censorship, 64
Sendak, Maurice, 63
sex trafficking legislation, 111-112
sexual abuse material, 27, 37-38
Shapiro, Ilya, 41
Sherlock Holmes stories, 92-93
SHIELD program, 73
Shorish, Y. L., 106
Smith, Christen A., 71-72
Smith College, 59-60
Snyder, Jeffrey Aaron, 47
The Social Construction of Reality (Berger and Luckmann), 9
Social History of Knowledge (Burke), 8
social justice, 6-7, 10, 12, 55, 105
social media, 17, 20, 36, 77, 78, 110-111, 113
societal change, 101-102
Society of American Archivists, 65, 104
sociology of knowledge, 7-9
Solove, Daniel, 70, 71-72, 74, 81, 118
Sova, Dawn B., 19, 66
The Speaker (film), 102-103

Special Library Association, 104
speech
    embeddedness of, 39-40, 42-45
    fighting words, 27, 37-39
    free, 1, 17, 37, 38, 41-42, 45-46, 47-48
    hateful or harmful, 25, 35-36, 42-45, 48, 114-115, 118
Spiegelman, Art, 63, 115
Springer, Nancy, 92-93
Squarespace, 76
Stamatakis, Katherine A., 57
state laws, 61-62
Stefancic, Jean, 115
Stop Enabling Sex Traffickers Act (SESTA), 111-112
Stoycheff, Elizabeth, 110
Strossen, Nadine, 39, 45, 48, 115
"Struggling to Breathe" (Gibson et al.), 106
Sturges, Paul, 4
Suber, Peter, 93, 95
sunshine laws, 61-62
Supreme Court, 23, 26-27, 38-39, 41, 45, 78, 89-90
surveillance, 70-71, 110, 112-113
Suu Kyi, Aung San, 44
Sye, David, 116

T

Taylor, Harriet, 21
Taylor, Natalie Greene, 66
tech companies, safe harbor for, 110-111
TERFs (transexclusionary radical feminists), 42
This Book Is Gay (Dawson), 63
This Film Is Not Yet Rated (Dick), 66
Tinker v. Des Moines Independent Community School District, 27
Tise, Ellen, 118
tracking, by Google, 112
trade secrets, 84-85
trademarks, 83, 84
Trump, Donald, 7, 42, 111, 113
Tushnet, Mark, 38
Twitter, 7, 20, 40, 113

U

United Nations, 2, 24-25, 60, 86
United Nations Universal Declaration of Human Rights, 2, 24-26, 28-29, 36, 37, 53, 84, 87
United States
    First Amendment of, 11, 26-28, 38-39, 115, 117
    history of copyright in, 85-89
    laws in, 26-28, 37-39, 43, 61-62, 76-77, 83-95, 110-112, 116-117
United States Copyright Office, 88, 95

United States Supreme Court, 23, 26-27, 38-39, 41, 78, 89-90
Universal Declaration of Human Rights, UN, 2, 24-26, 28-29, 36, 37, 53, 84, 87
User Privacy (Connolly), 79
utilitarianism, 21, 22, 23

V

values vs. morals, 10, 103-104
Villasenor, Maya, 111
Virginia v. Black, 39
vision statements, 58
visual art, 40, 63, 85, 93

W

Wade, Carrie, 46
Warburton, Nigel, 22
Ward, David V., 24
Webster, Noah, 86
Wedgeworth, Robert, 103
Wengert, Robert, 104
"Why You Can't Censorproof Your Public Library" (Schrader), 107
Wiegand, Shirley A., 31
Wiegand, Wayne A., 31
Wikipedia, 80, 113
Wiley, Ralph, 18
Words That Wound (Matsuda et al.), 43, 48
World Intellectual Property Organization (WIPO), 83, 84-85, 86, 89, 95
Wyatt, Anna May, 77-78, 80
Wynn, Natalie, 40

Y

Yates, Ella, 102
Yiannopoulos, Milo, 41
York, Jillian C., 112
Young Adult Literature, Libraries, and Conservative Activism (Gaffney), 66

Z

Zemke, Deborah, 87-88
Zuboff, Shoshana, 71

You may also be interested in...

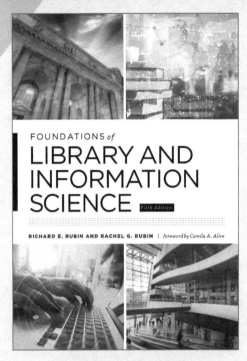

ISBN: 978-0-8389-4744-9

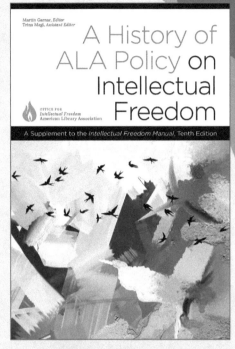

ISBN: 978-0-8389-3787-7

ISBN: 978-0-8389-1802-9

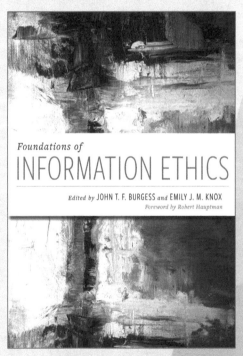

ISBN: 978-0-8389-1722-0

For more titles, visit **alastore.ala.org**